Wanderings

Works by Norwich Arts Center Artists

Other Books of Art from

New London Librarium

Mother Goose and Other Rhymes: Artists at Sayles School

Art of Love: Paintings by Colleen Hennessy, Thoughts from Rubem Alves

Selfies: Paintings by Wells Moore

By Night or Day: Paintings by Colleen Hennessy

Wheresoe'er: Paintings by Colleen Hennessy

Every Common Sight: Paintings by Colleen Hennessy

On Women: Paintings by Colleen Hennessy

Earth and Sky: Nature Meditations in Word and Water Color
(Judy Benson and Roxanne Steed)

Juner's Home: Paintings by Yujuan Patnode

Cultivating Illuminations: Paintings by Mark Patnode

Carefully Everywhere Descending: Paintings,
Photography, and Design by Glenn Alan Cheney

Dedicated to

Thom and Dee Keaney

with deep thanks for many years of kindness, friendship, and support of Norwich Arts Center

Wanderings: Works by Norwich Arts Center Artists

Written, edited and designed by Glenn Alan Cheney

Copyright © 2023 Norwich Arts Center

All artists presented herein retain all rights to and ownership of their works. No part of this book may be reproduced in any medium or format without the express permission of one of the copyright holder and the artist(s).

Front cover art, Winter, by Yujuan Patnode. Back cover art, The Good Old Days, by Rita Dawley

Published by
New London Librarium
Hanover, CT 06350
NLLibrarium.com

ISBN: 978-1-947074-71-2

Wanderings

Works by Norwich Arts Center Artists

New London Librarium

Introduction

When did art start?

Half a million years ago somebody engraved an image on a shell. A few hundred thousand years later, a visionary Neanderthal seems to have tinkered with eight eagle talons to fashion jewelry. A hundred thousand years later, people were painting on cave walls.

Forty thousand years later–1987 to be exact–a handful of artists, activists and appreciators decided that Norwich, Connecticut, needed to get its arts organized with some kind of registry of artists and a calendar of events. The group founded the Norwich Arts Council. Soon, in the way of artists who are always looking a little further than everyone else, the group fell into a bigger dream, a home for the arts in downtown Norwich.

They found such a place in a 19th-century temperance hall at 60 Broadway, just across a plaza from City Hall. It was a perfect spot for what would become Norwich Arts Center. It had two storefronts, rentable office space upstairs, and a theater–or rather, a wreck of a theater–on the top floor. The stage had held everything from temperance meetings to vaudeville acts to boxing matches, but it had yet to see its final act.

The dream was to open an arts center co-op, a place where all forms of art–visual, musical, theatrical–by all sorts of artists–old, young, amateur, professional, the demonstrably crazy, the marginally sane–could carry on the very human urge to create something beautiful.

The ground floor had served as a beauty salon, a coffeeshop and a bar, but it was empty in 1987. The owners, an enlightened couple with a vision that exceeded mere revenue, were willing to lease the place, and later sell it, at below-market prices.

Market price in downtown Norwich was then and still is a questionable issue. Real estate isn't necessarily worth what it's worth. Businesses come and go, alas more often closing than opening. Magnificent buildings remain empty. Few businesses that were open in 1987 are still there. But the arts remain.

The survival of art over commerce–of beauty over utility–says much about the human urge to create and to experience creation. Commerce involves creation, but it is burdened by ulterior motives. Art comes into being for its own sake, the sake of beauty.

Art is intrinsically human. It is part of what distinguishes humans from other species. It touches the human soul. It brings us together. It hints of truth, beauty, love, and the ephemerality of life. We don't understand where art comes from or how it touches us so deeply. Part of the beauty of art is in that inexplicable mystery, that mystery as inexplicable as the soul.

Whatever it is that's been passed down to us since Neanderthal times, it has been holding its own in downtown Norwich for over 35 years. Despite the economic shifts from downtowns to malls and then to the internet, Norwich Arts Center has stood as an enduring pillar of the downtown area.

This book celebrates not just art and artists but the spirit that helps keep Norwich vibrant and, in its own way, beautiful. The artists whose work appears herein aren't necessarily residents of Norwich, but, as members of Norwich Arts Center, they are part of the city's soul. They came to Norwich to share their art, and this book has been created for that same purpose.

Glenn Alan Cheney
Hanover, Conn.

The Artists

Debora Aldo

Glynis J. Blanker

Virginia Chase

Glenn Alan Cheney

Karen Coombs

Rita Dawley

Mark Dixon

Michael Dubenetsky

Carol Dunn

Blaney Harris

Sandra Jeknavorian

Susan Scott Kenney

Melody Knight Leary

Gerlinde Lehner

Mary Ann Lewis

Gabe Lipman

Susan Masse

Lori Neumann

Marianne Nicholas

Susan Parish

Mark Patnode

Yujuan Patnode

Lori Rembetski

Lisa Shasha

Gretchen van der Lyke

Gabrielle Zane

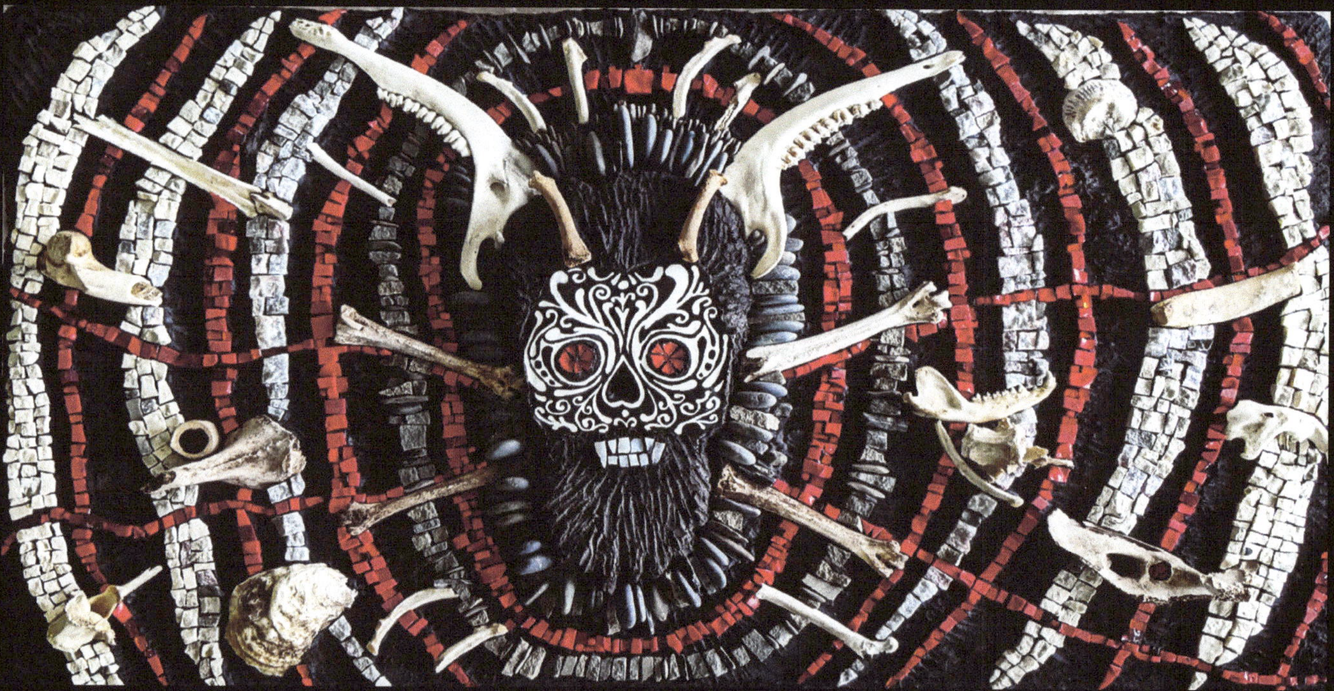

Debora Aldo, YOU-cifer: Bones of Contention, mosaic with bone and carvings

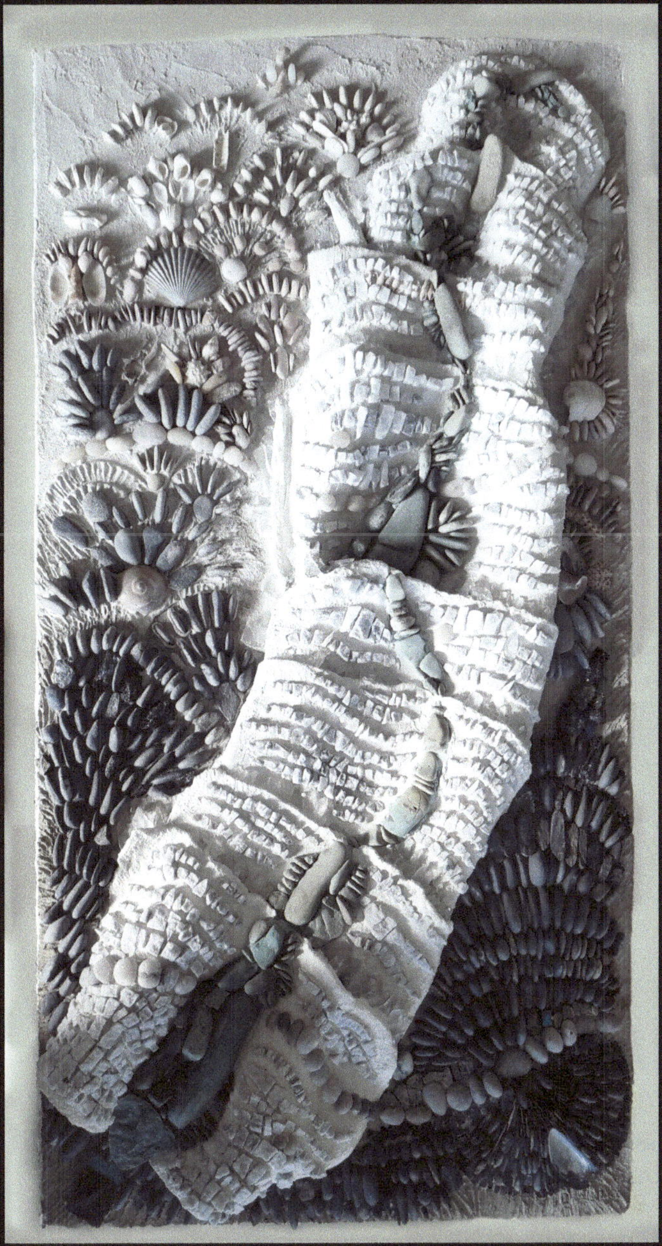

Debora Aldo, Ascension, mosaic on substrate

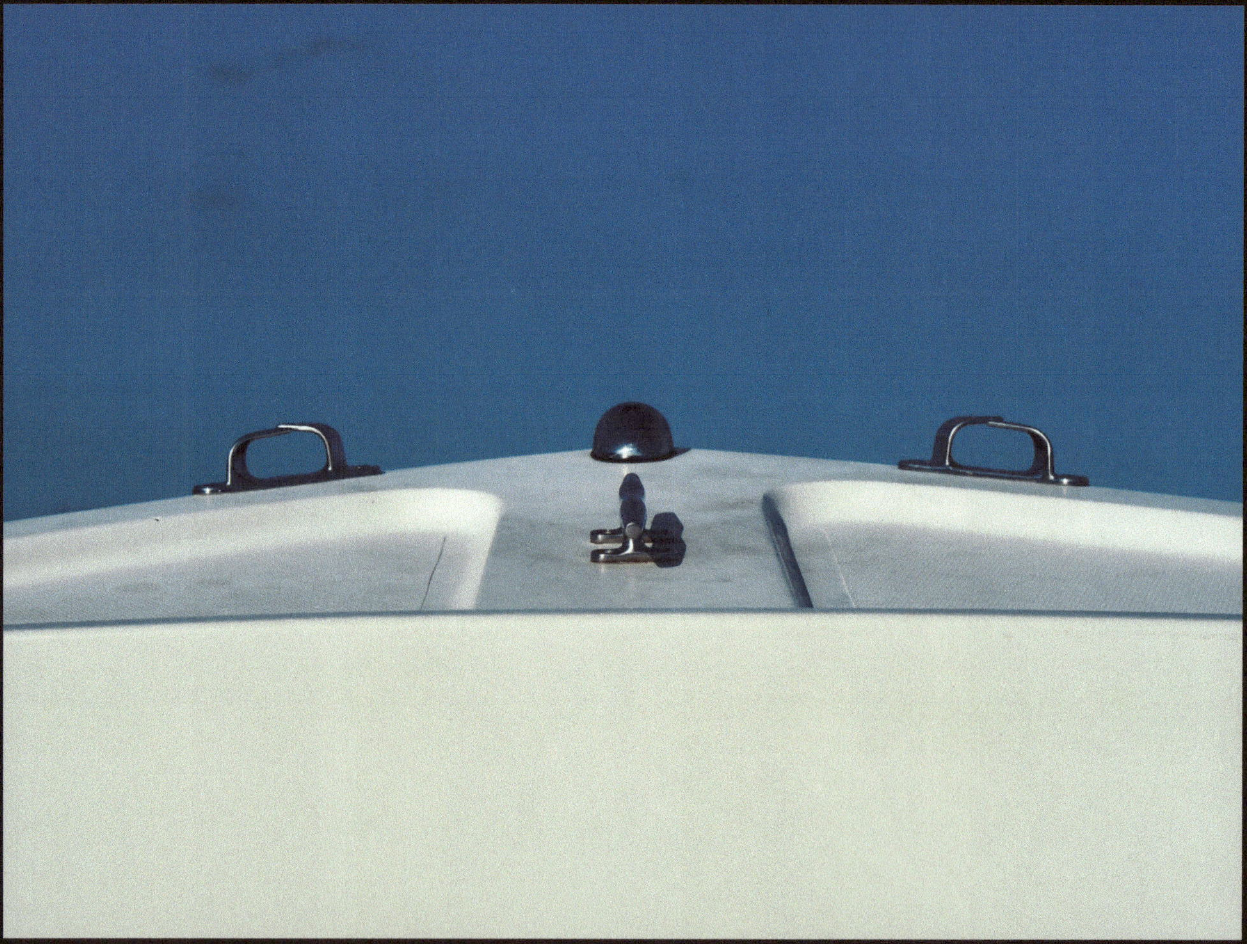

Glynis J. Blanker, Digital Cool, photograph

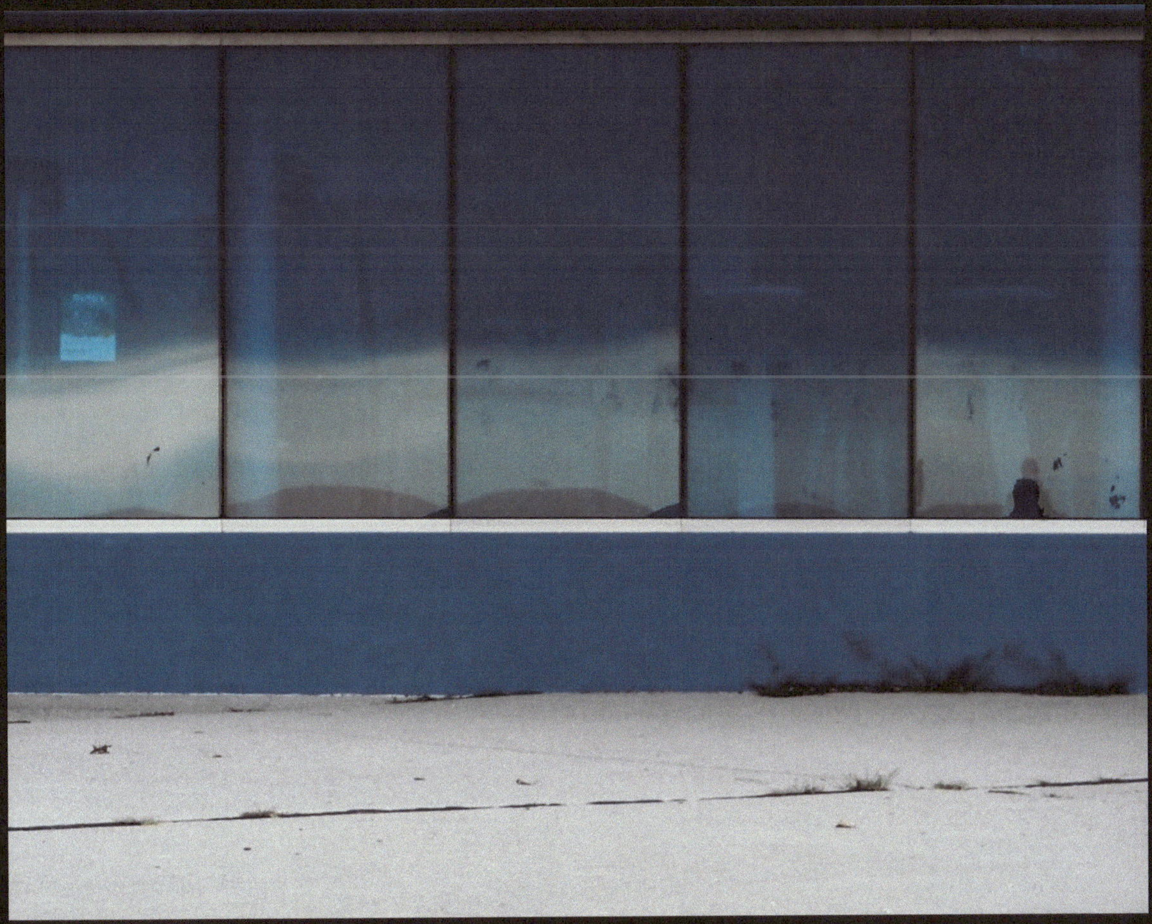

Glynis J. Blanker, Ocean Beach, photograph

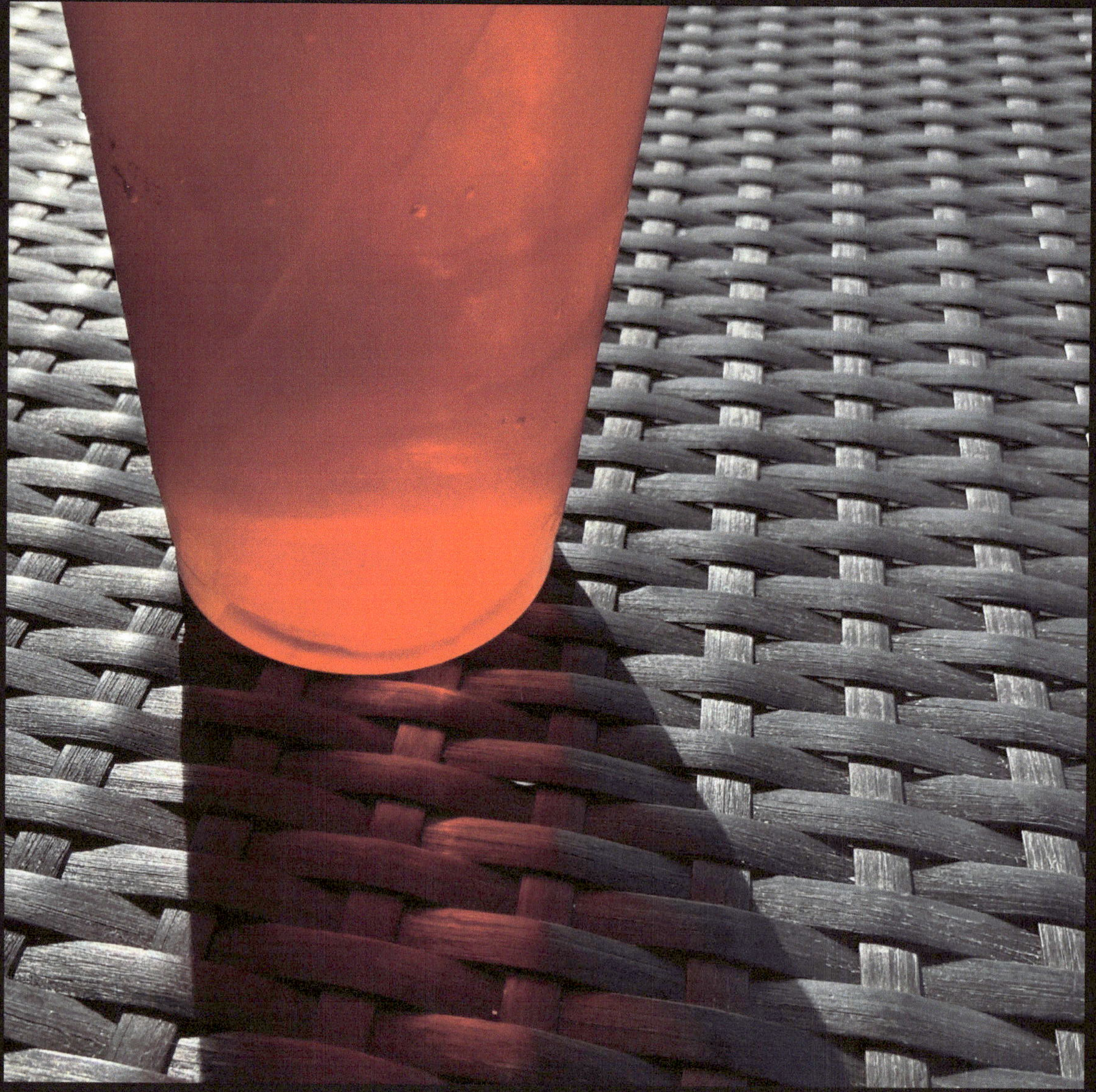

Glynis J. Blanker, Raspberry Red, photograph

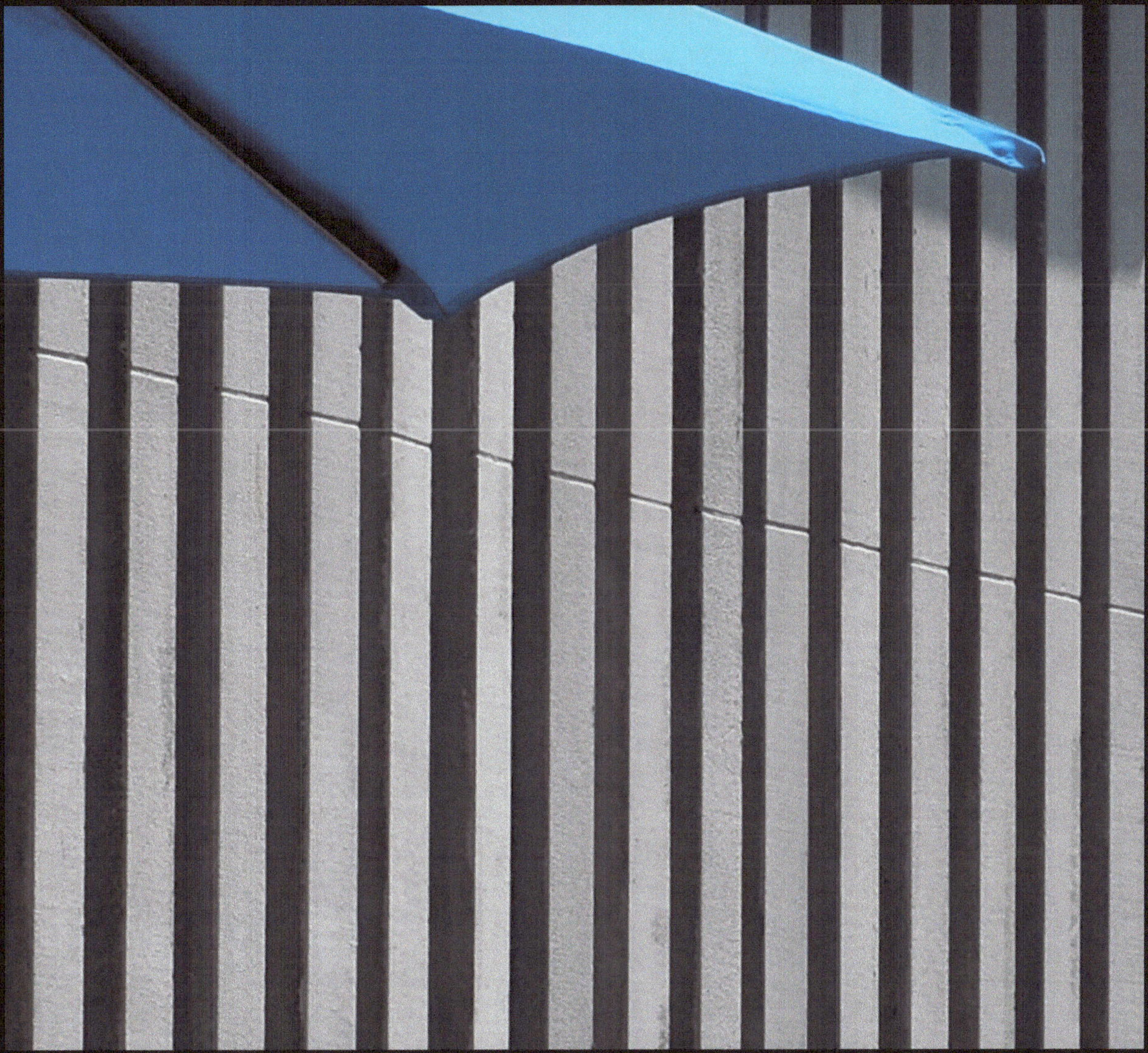

Glynis J. Blanker, Untitled, photograph

Virginia Chase, Colors of Sunset, photograph

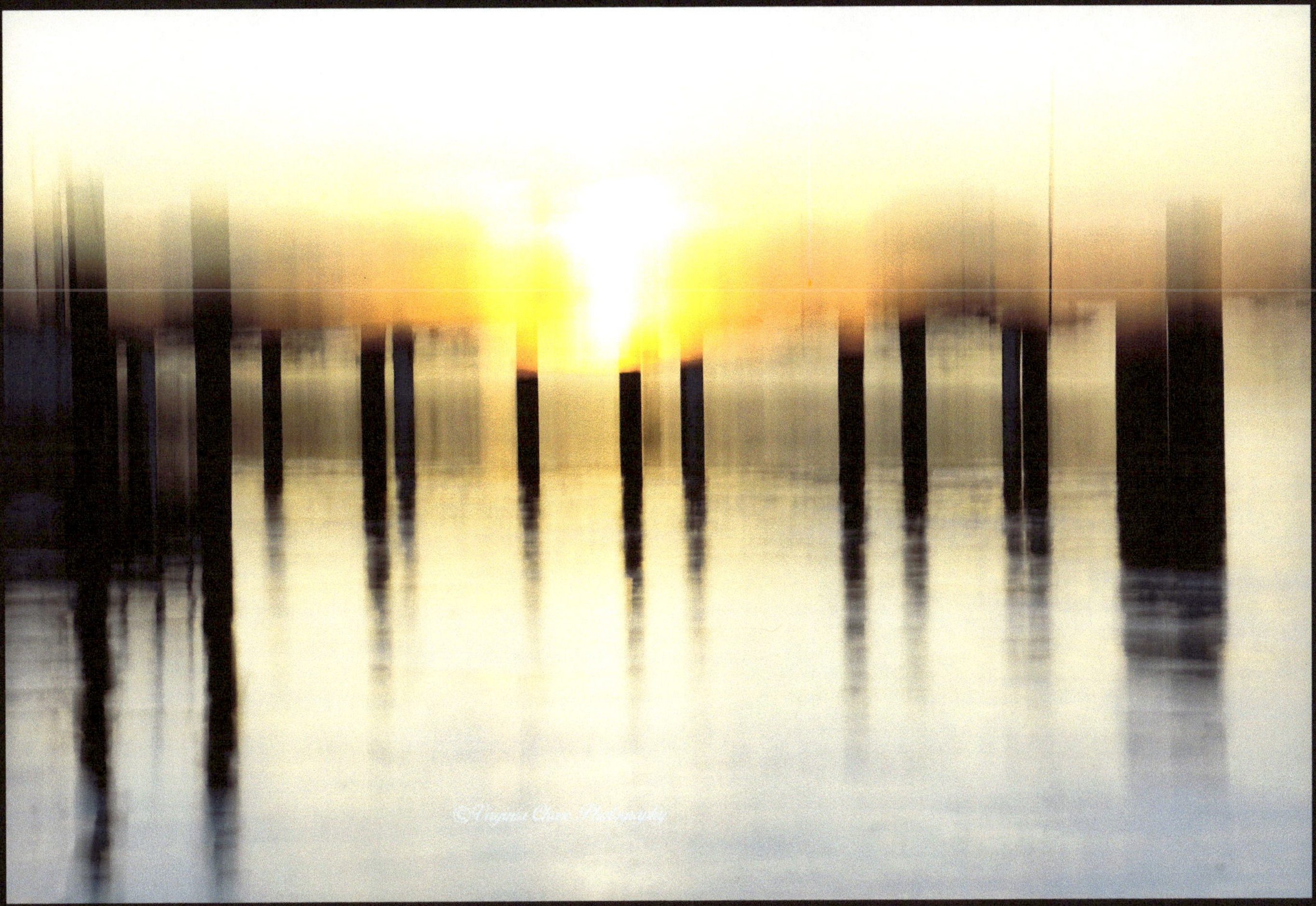

Virginia Chase, Westerly Marina, photograph

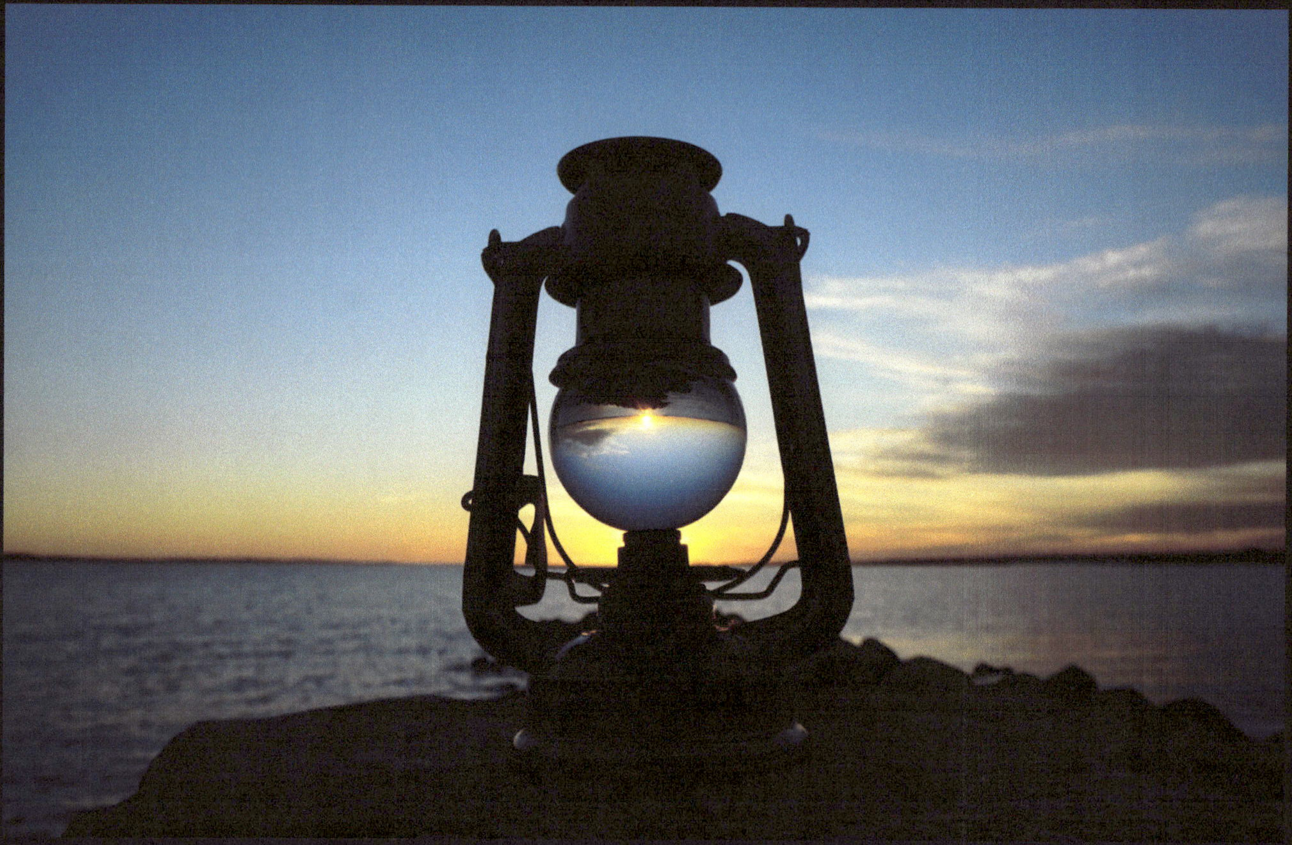

Virginia Chase, Stonington Point Sunset, photograph

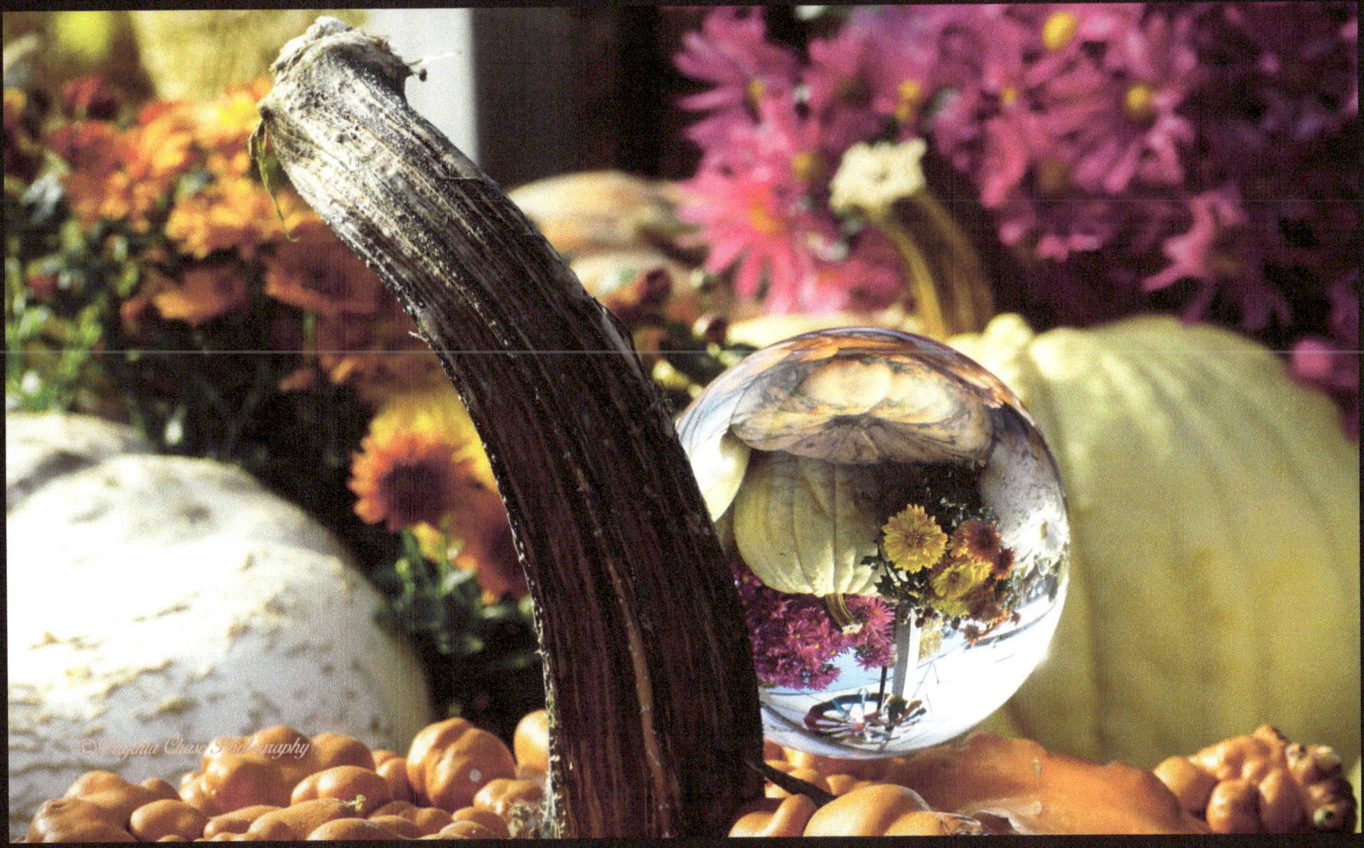

Virginia Chase, Autumn Lensball, photograph

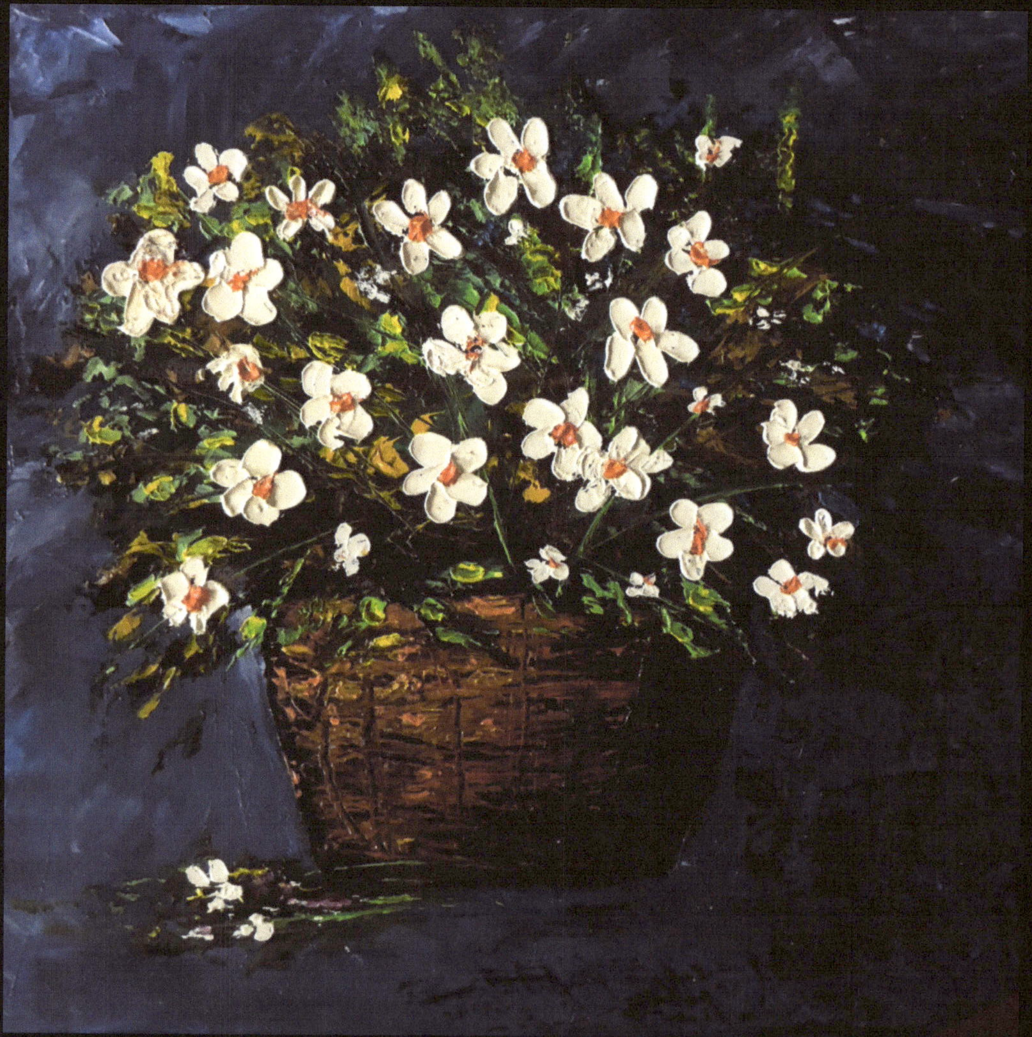

Glenn Alan Cheney, Happy Basket, acrylic on canvas

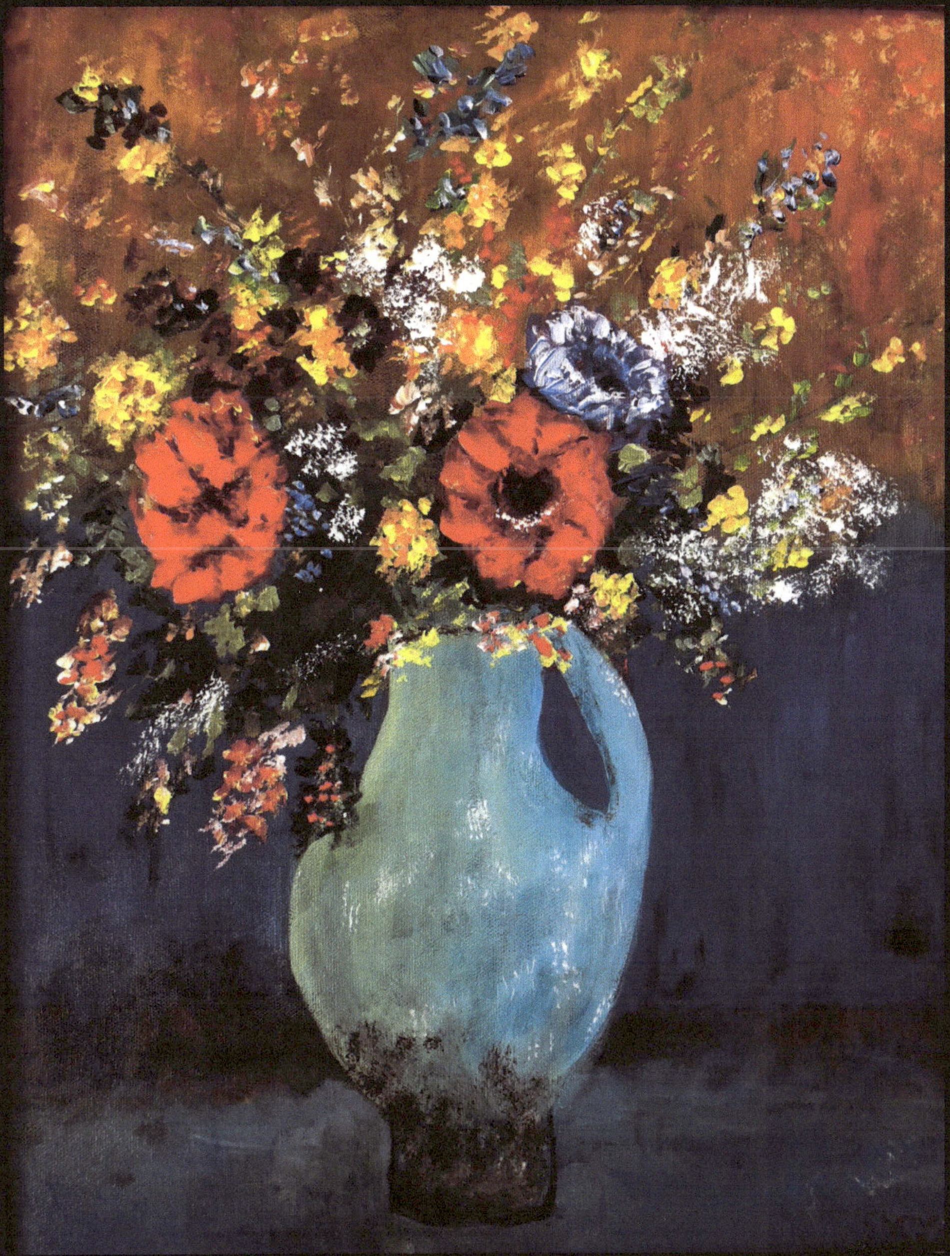

Glenn Alan Cheney, Bouquet in Autumn Light, acrylic on canvas

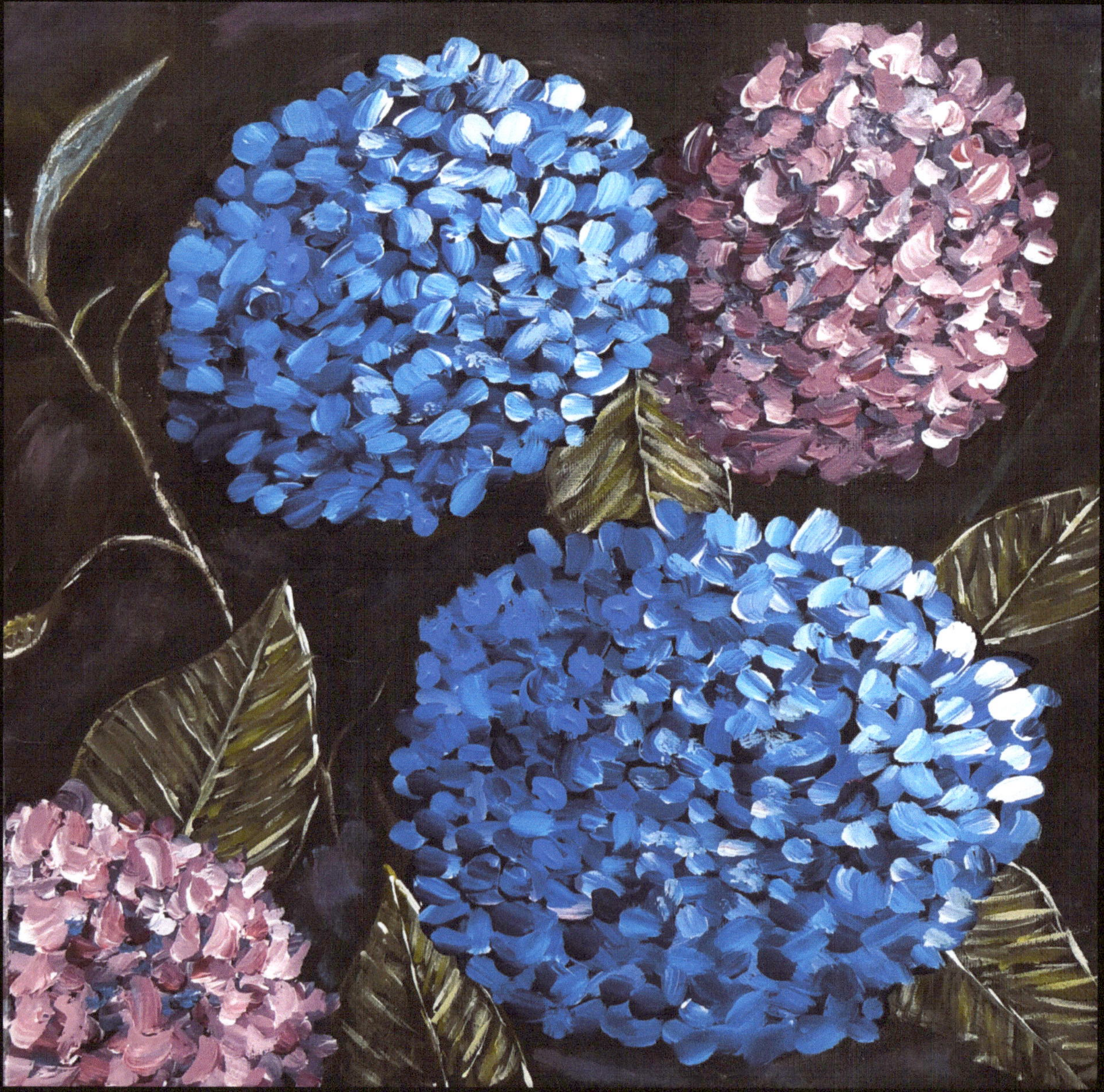

Glenn Alan Cheney, Hortensias, acrylic on canvas

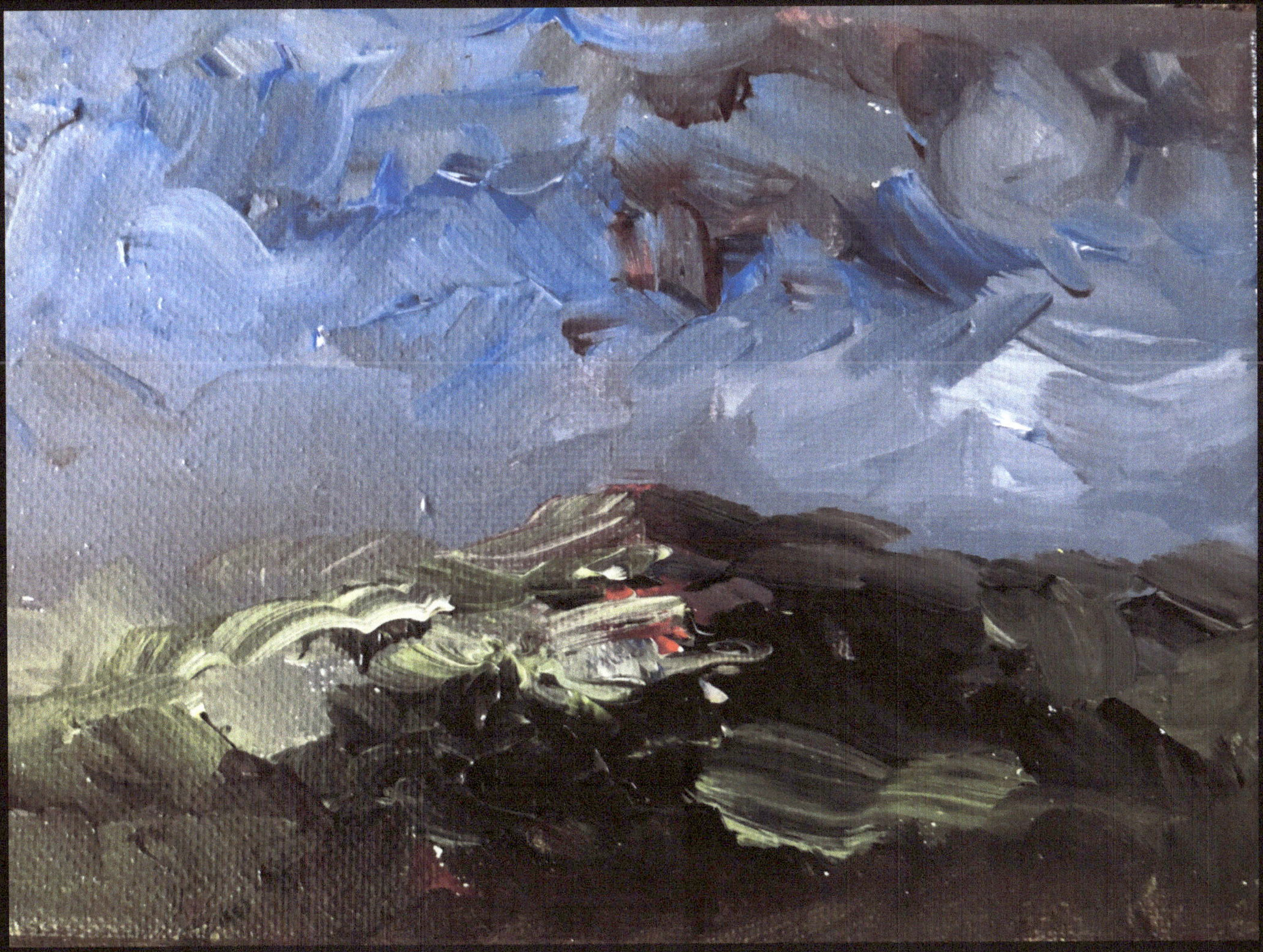

Glenn Alan Cheney, Red Mystery, acrylic on canvas

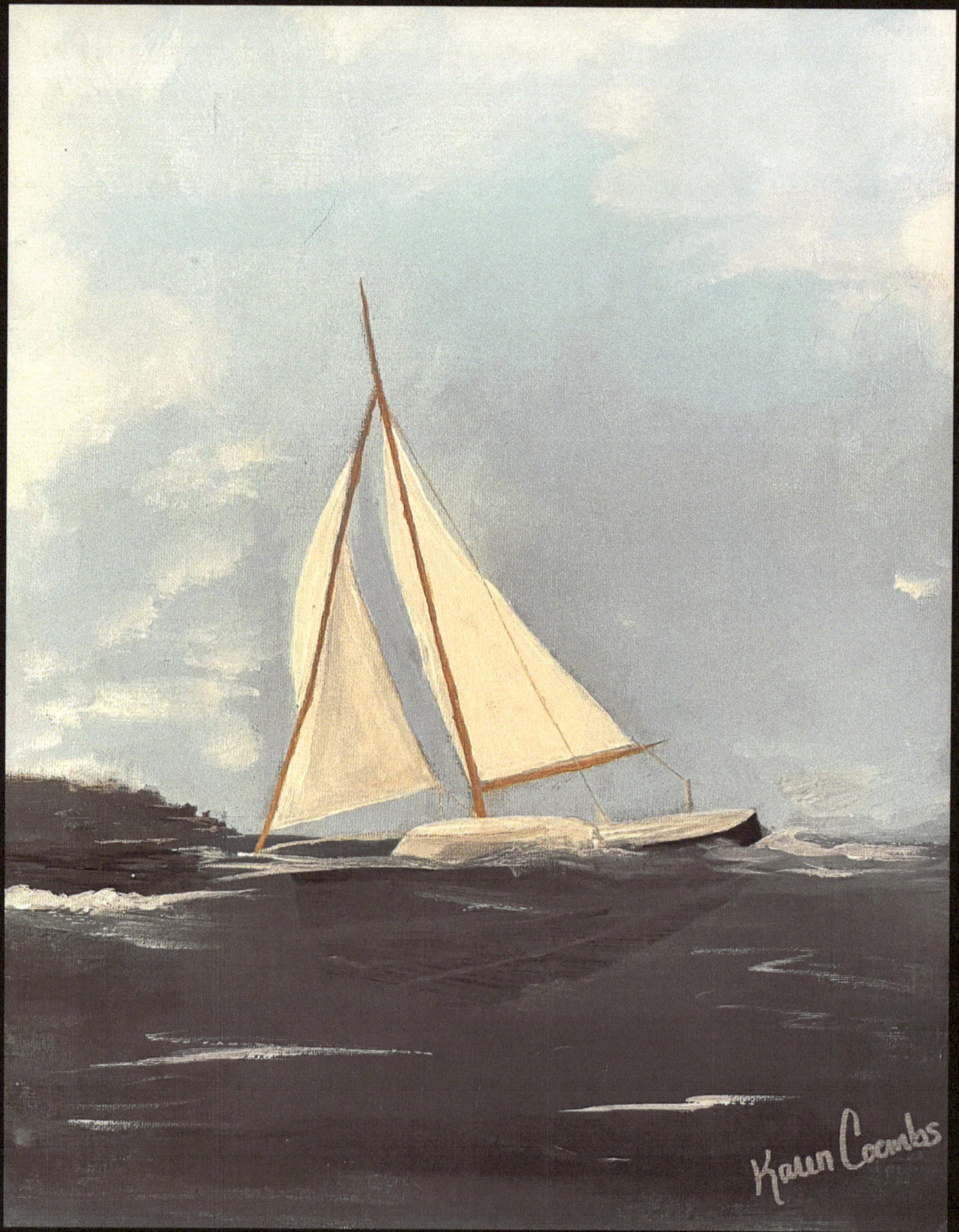

Karen Coombs, Hole in Water, acrylic on canvas

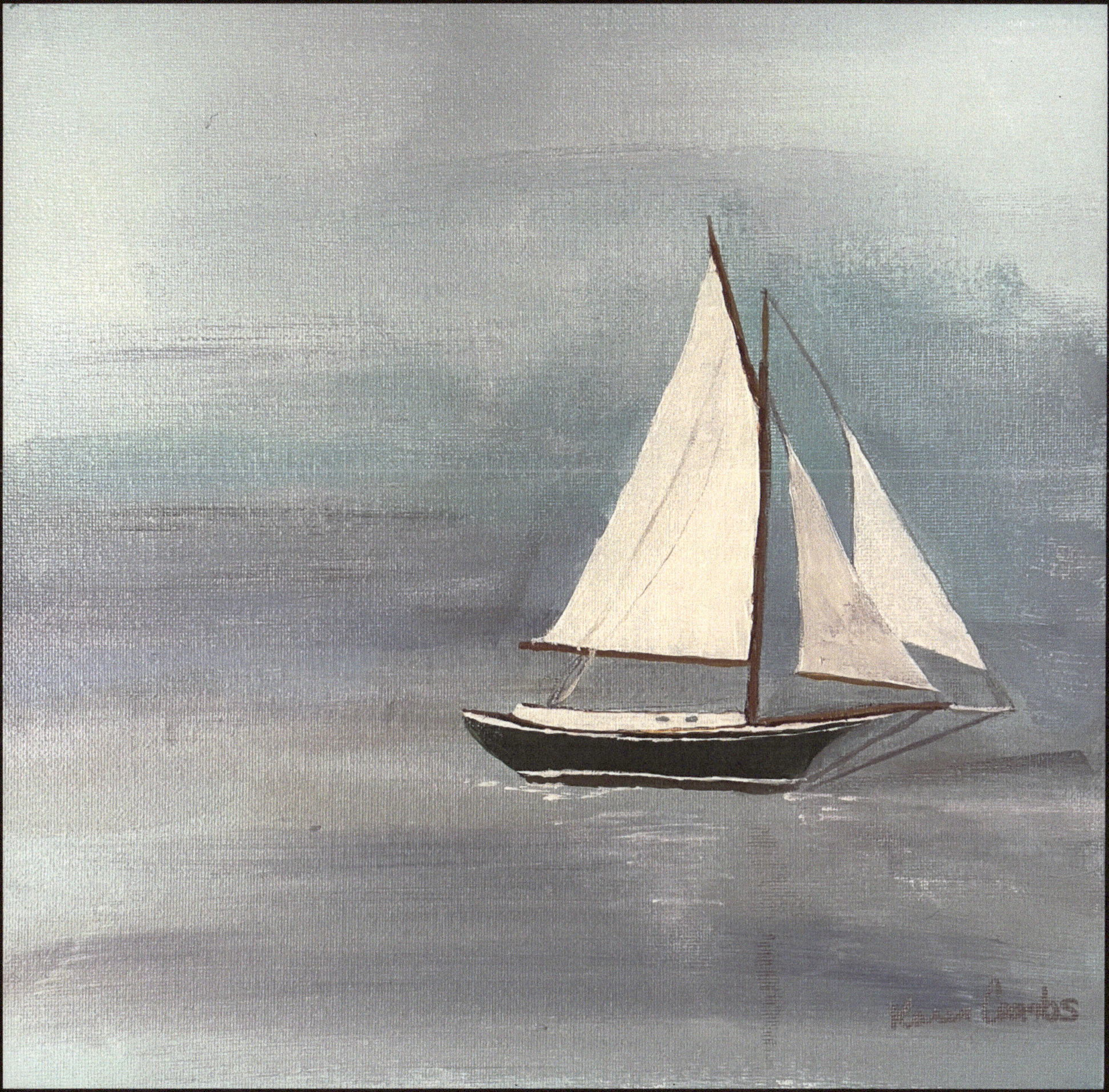

Karen Coombs, Boat in Fog, acrylic on canvas

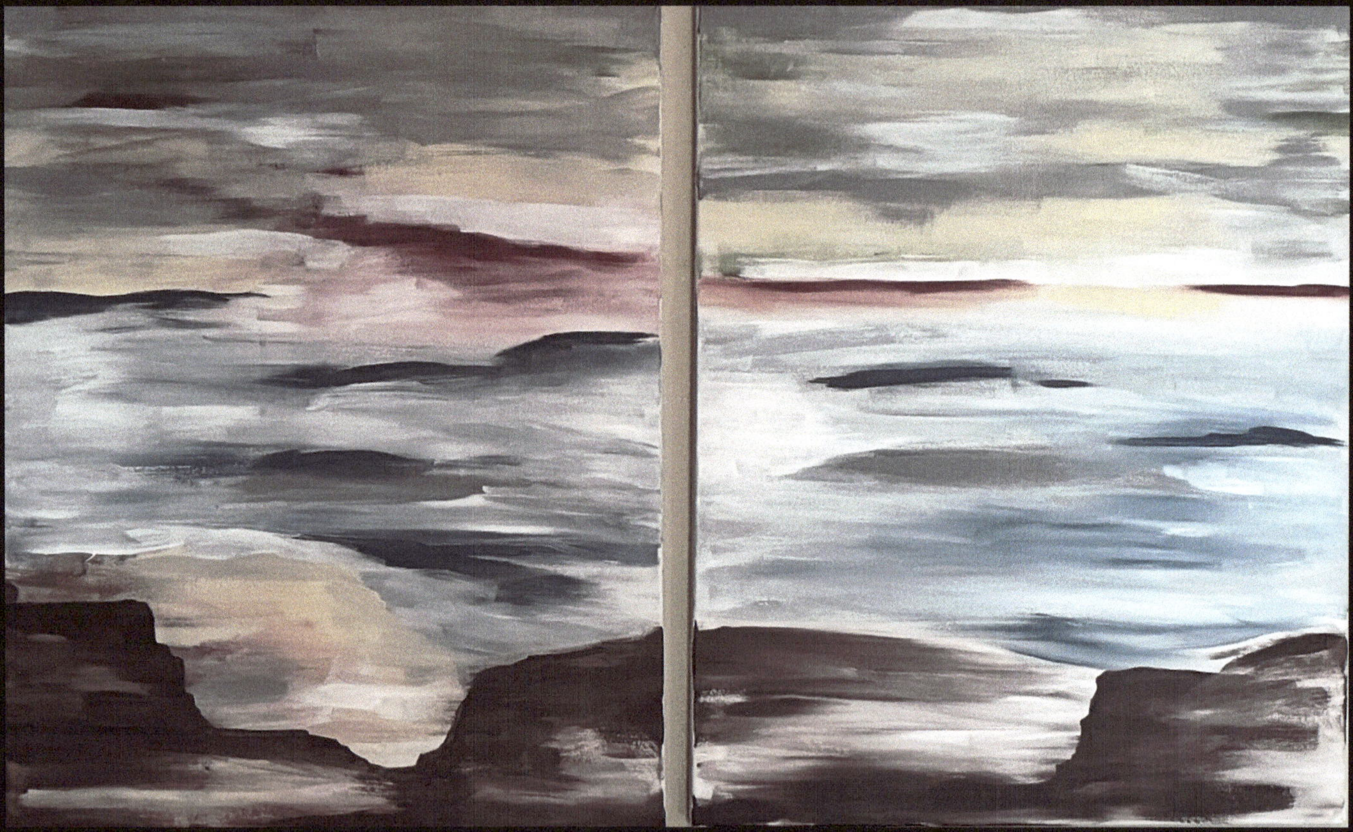

Karen Coombs, Cliff Walk, acrylic on canvas

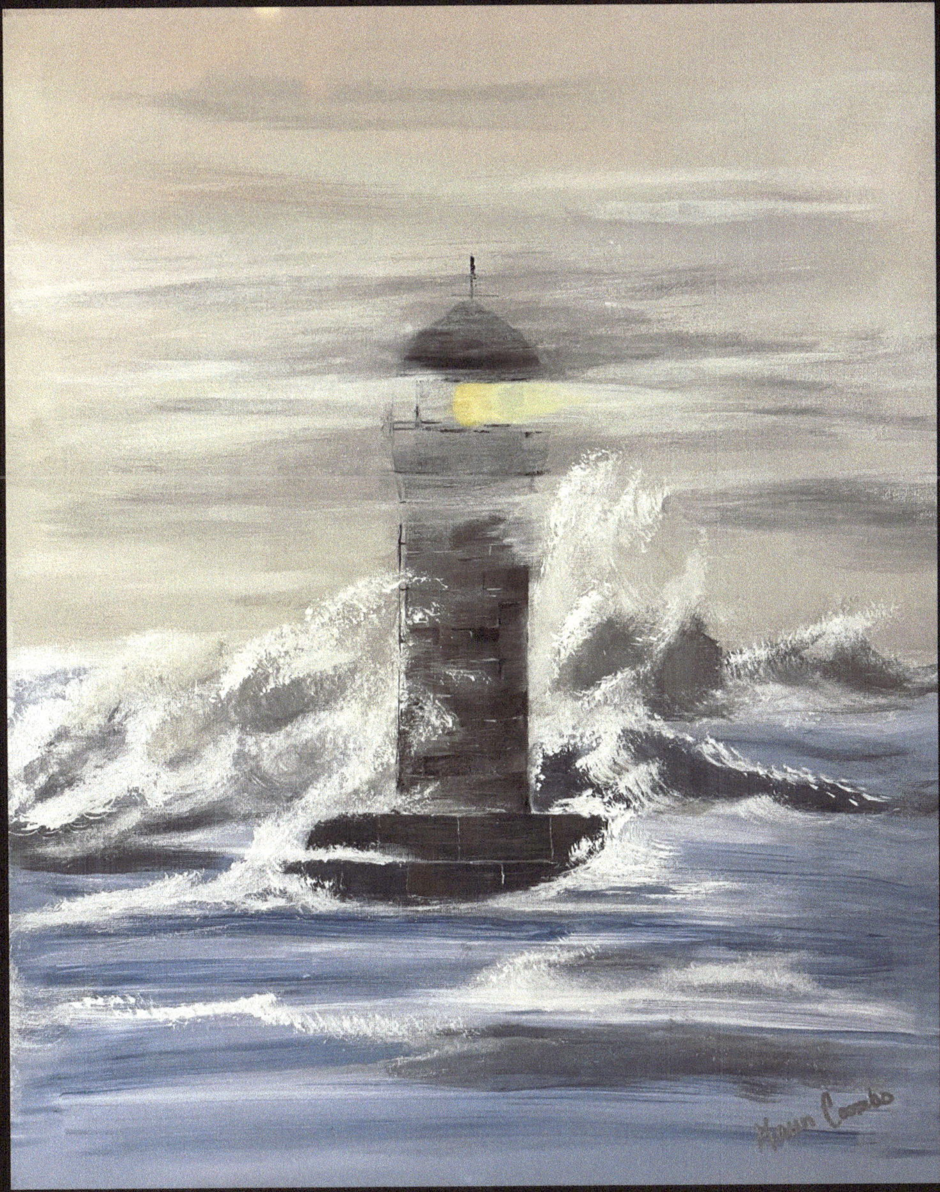

Karen Coombs, Lighthouse in Storm, acrylic on canvas

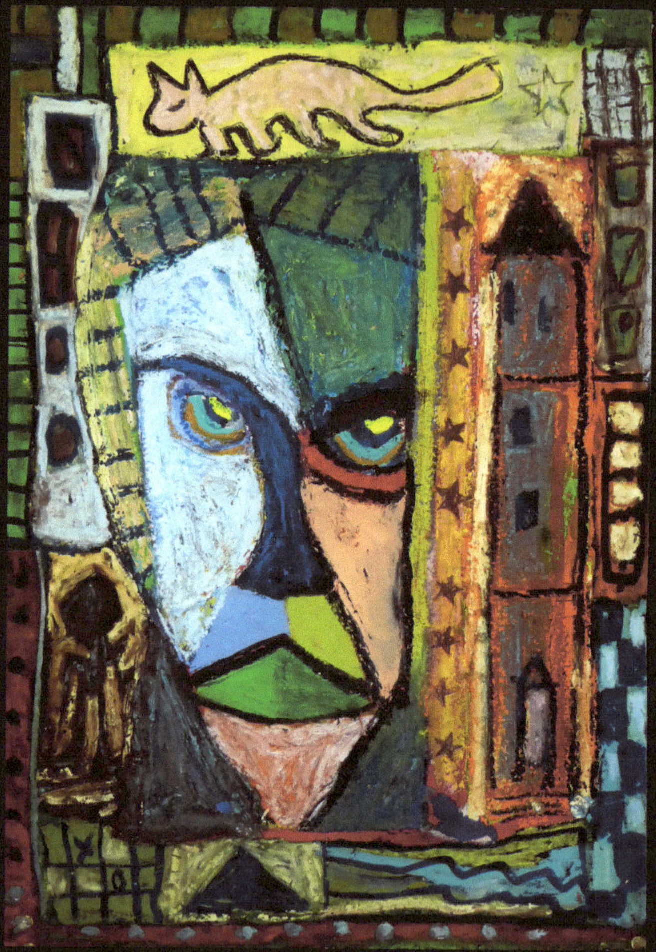

Rita Dawley, Make My Day, pastel on paper

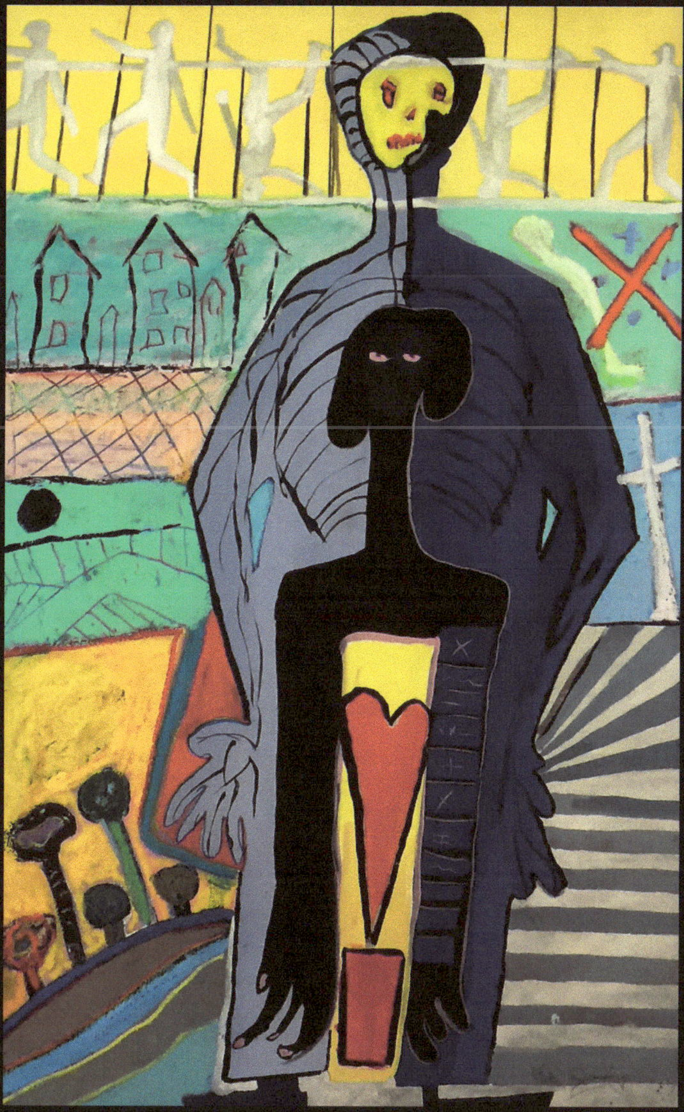

Rita Dawley, Isolated Couple, pastel on paper

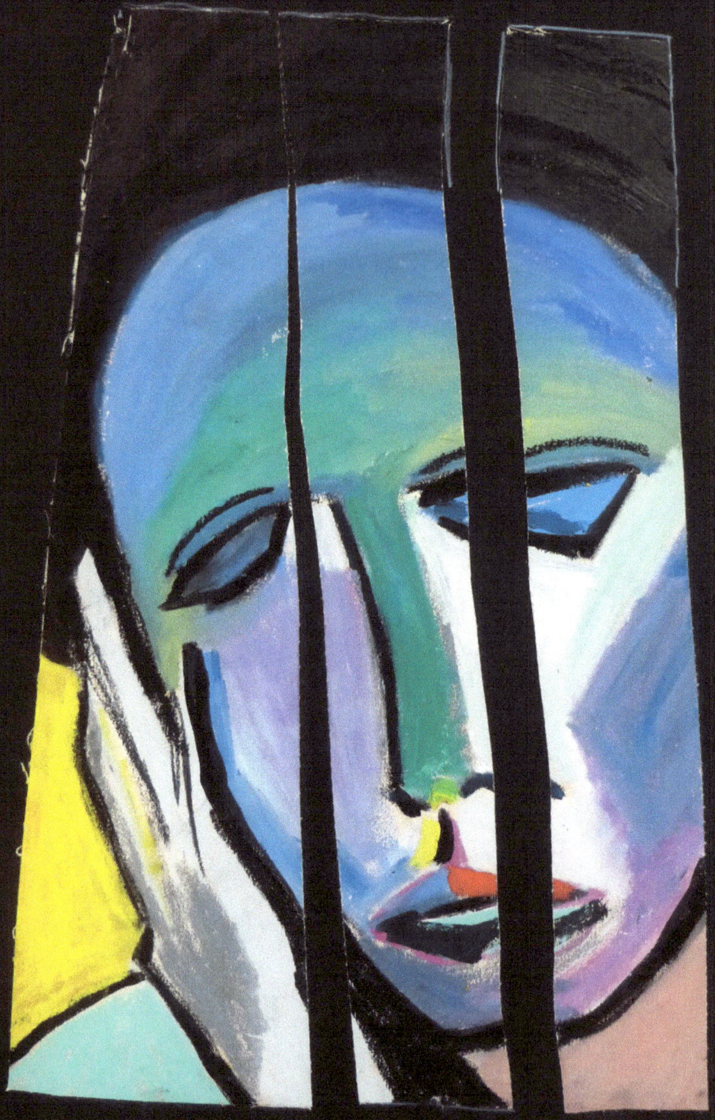

Rita Dawley, Blue Face, pastel on paper

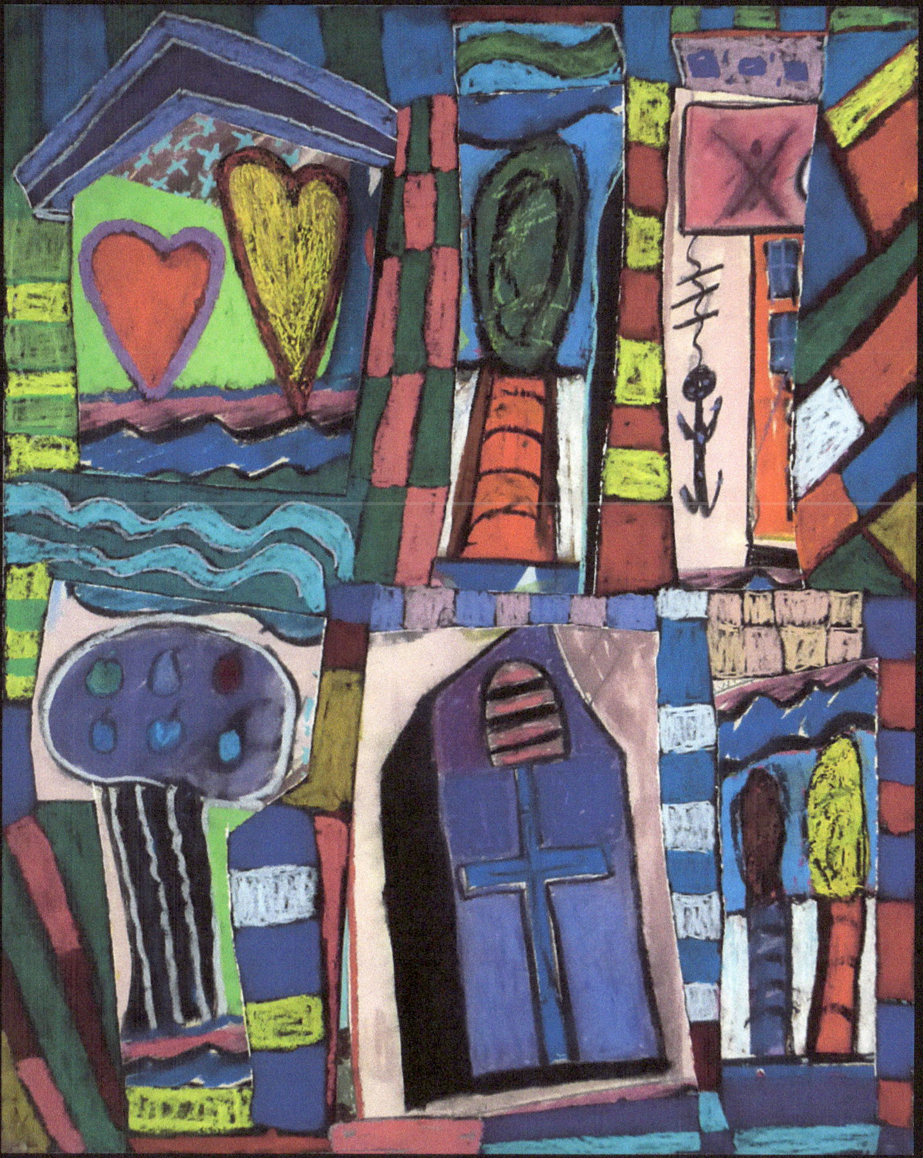

Rita Dawley, The Good Old Days, pastel on paper

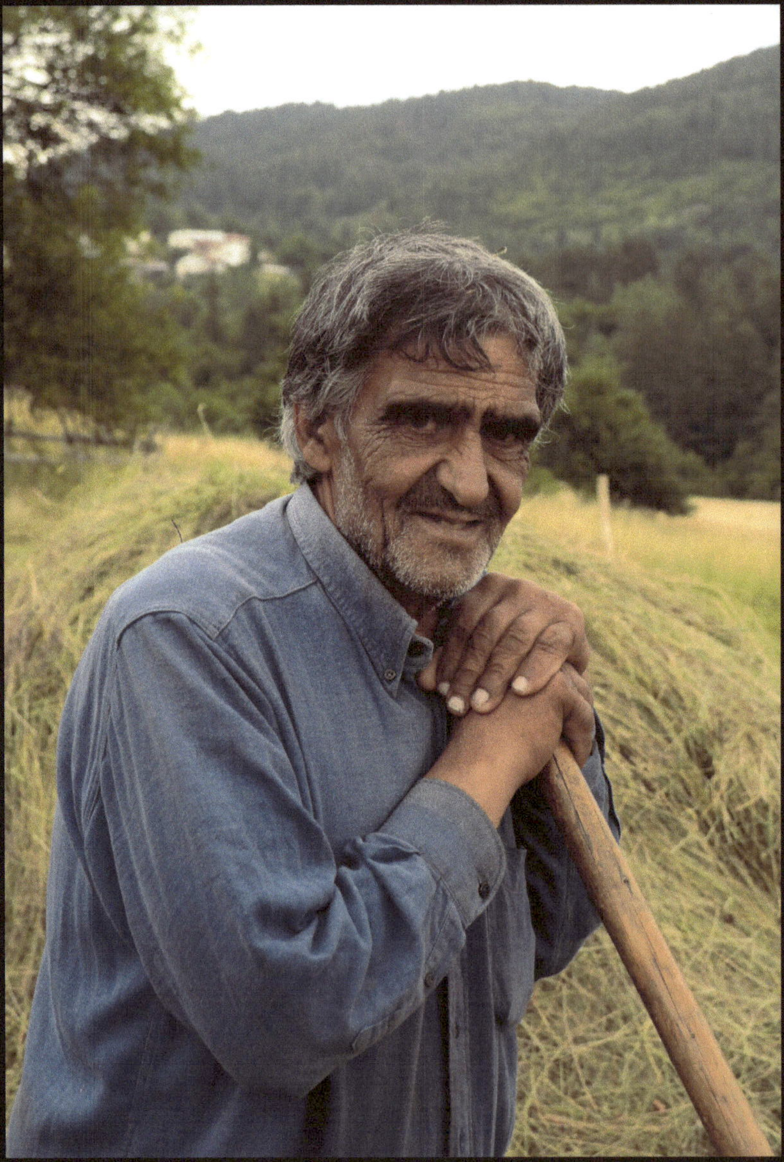

Mark Dixon, Roma Farmer, photograph

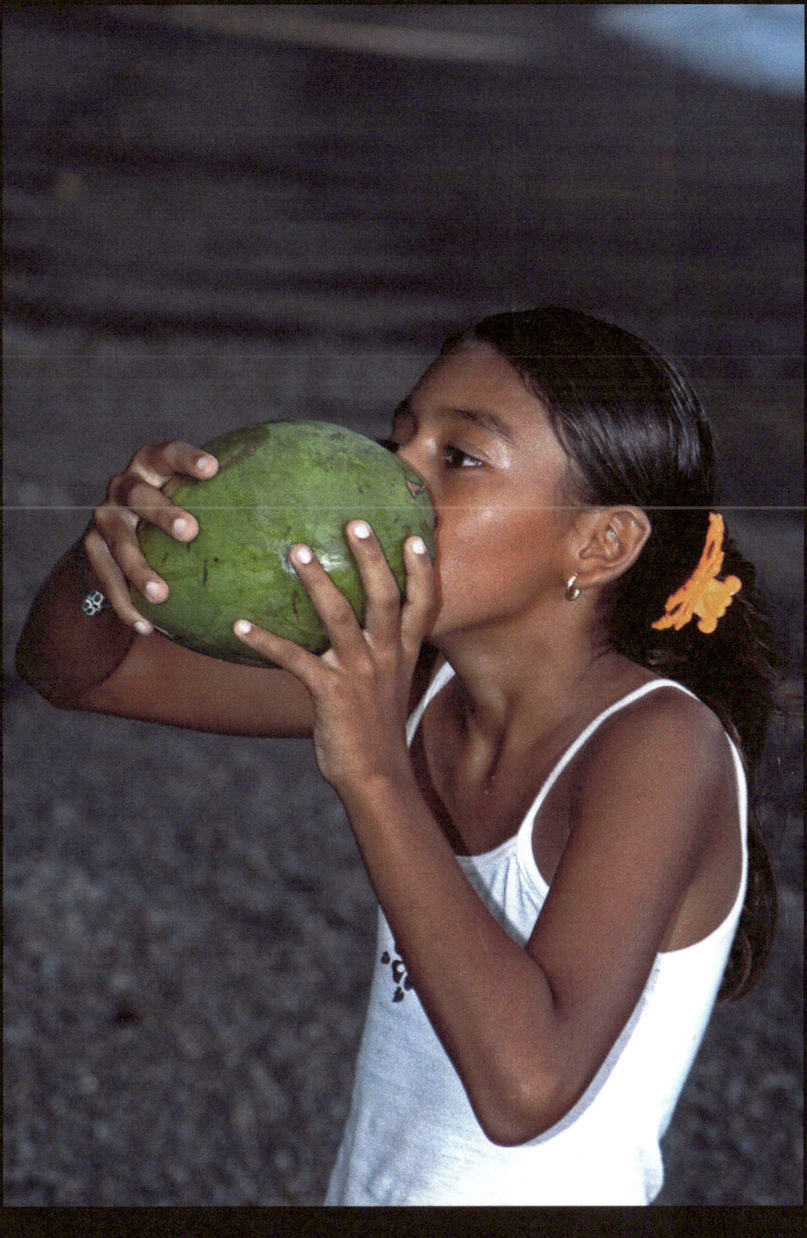

Mark Dixon, Pipa Girl, photograph

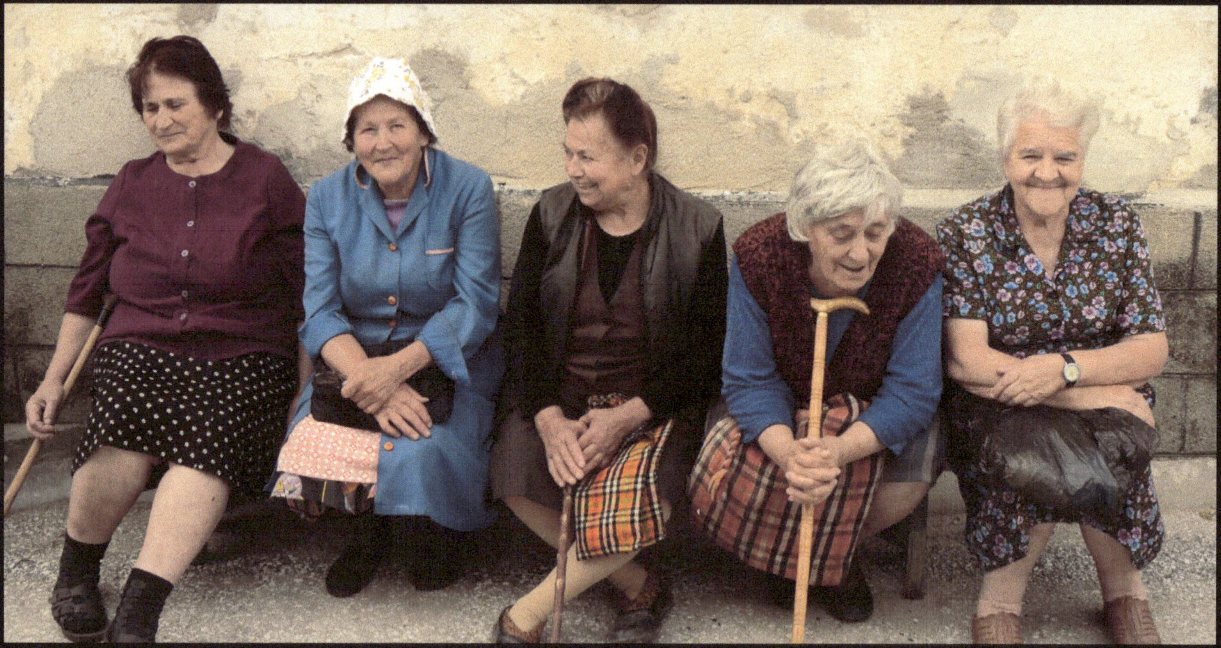

Mark Dixon, Town Meeting, photograph

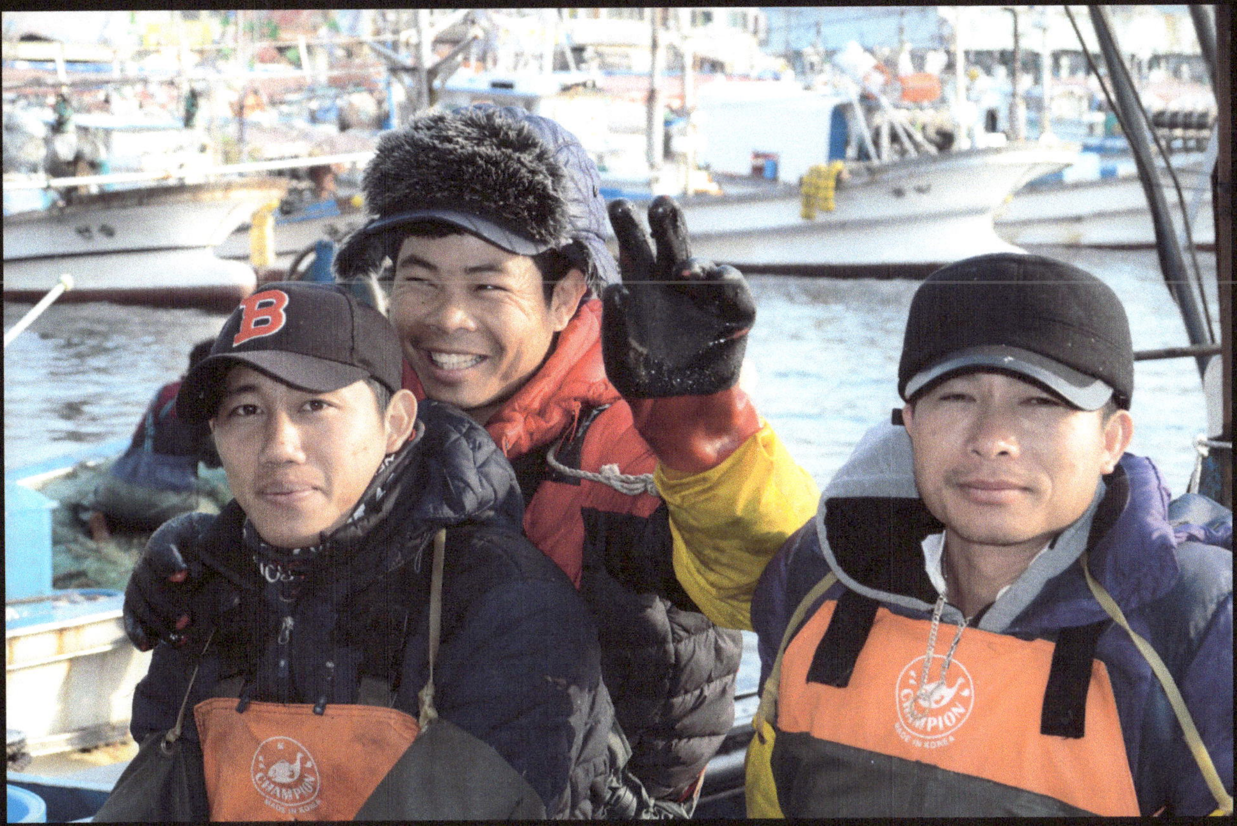

Mark Dixon, Young Fishermen in a Foreign Port, photograph

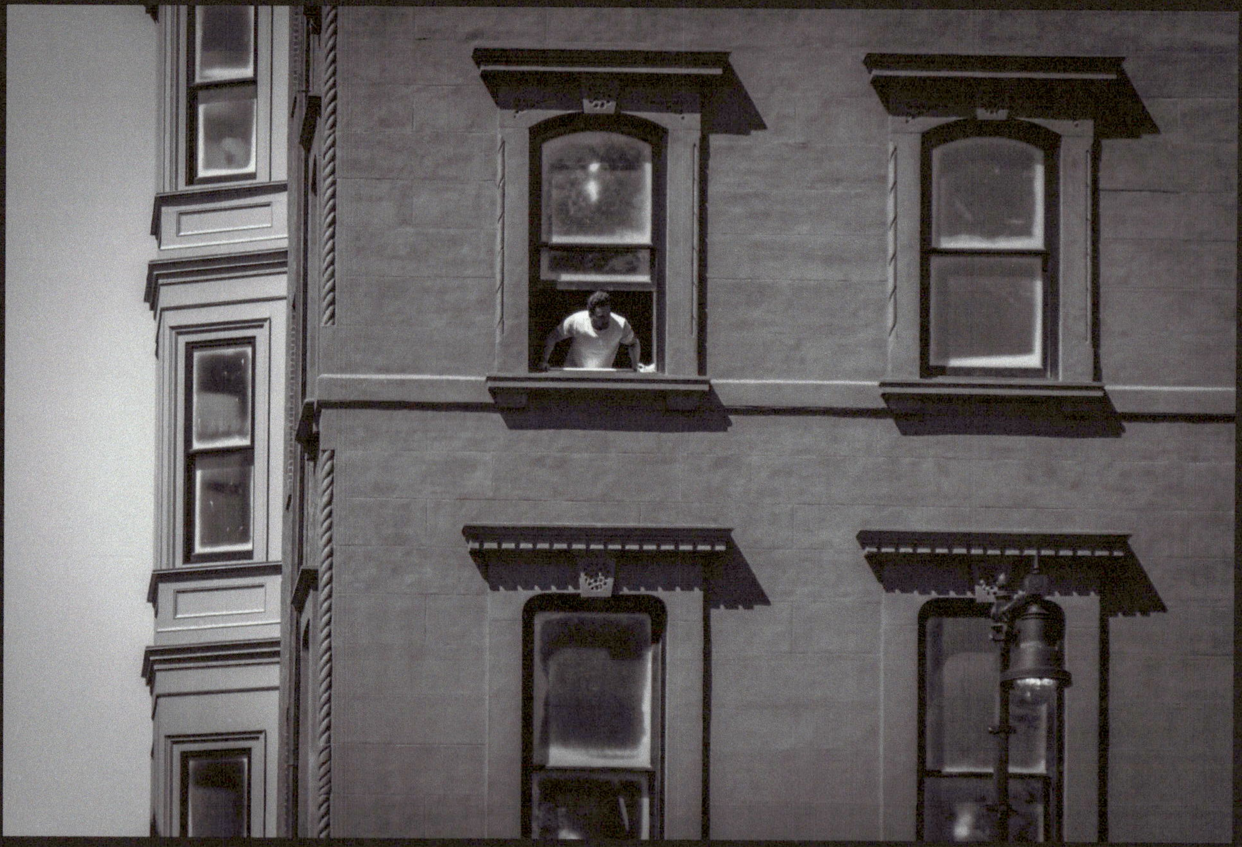

Michael Dubenetsky, Brownstone, photograph

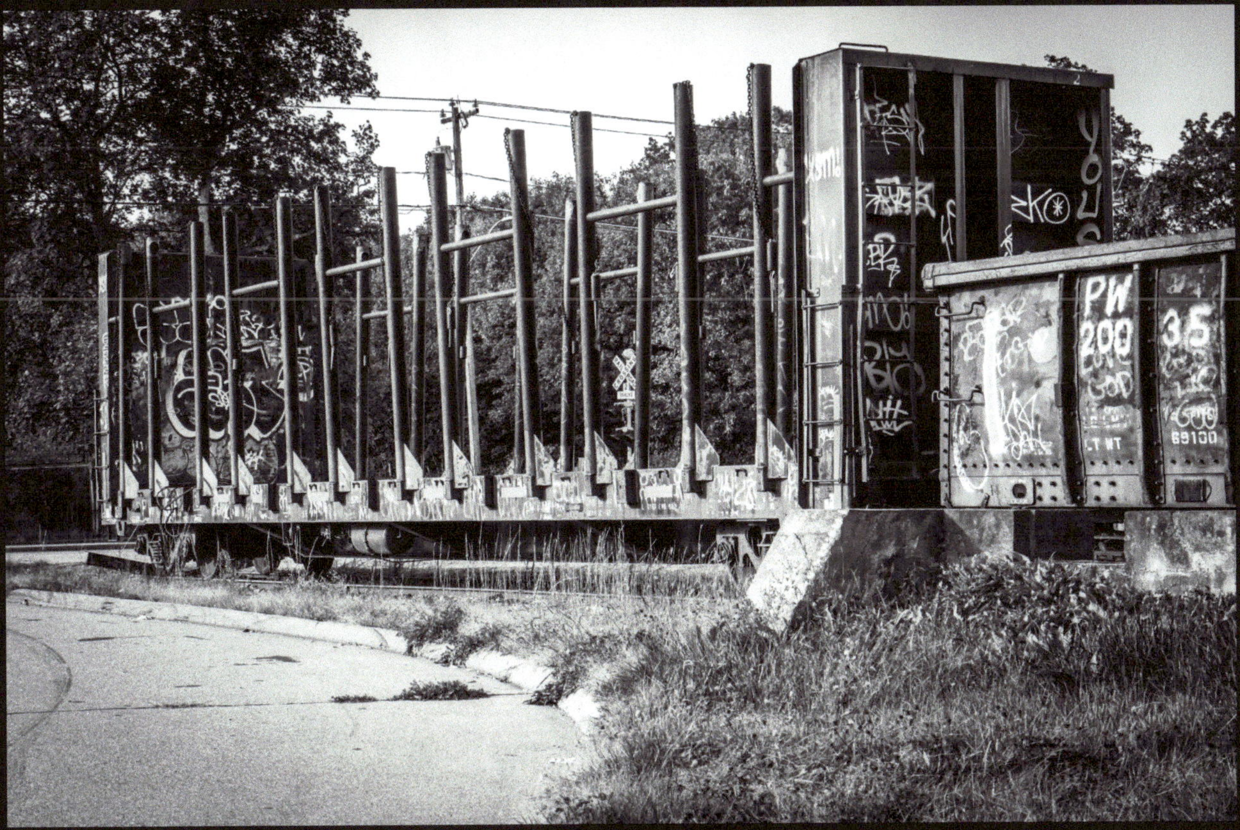

Michael Dubenetsky, Forgotten, photograph

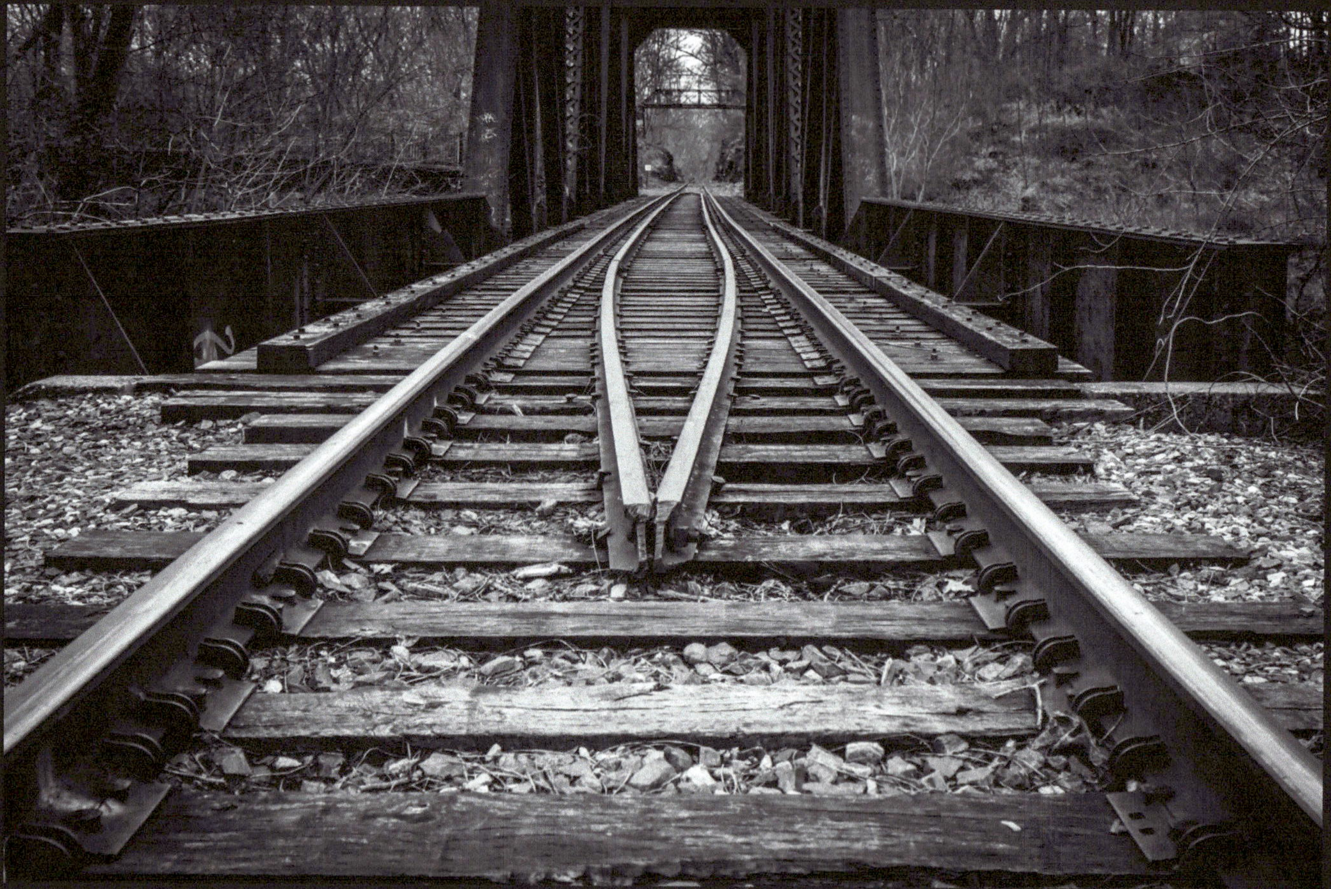

Michael Dubenetsky, Tracks, photograph

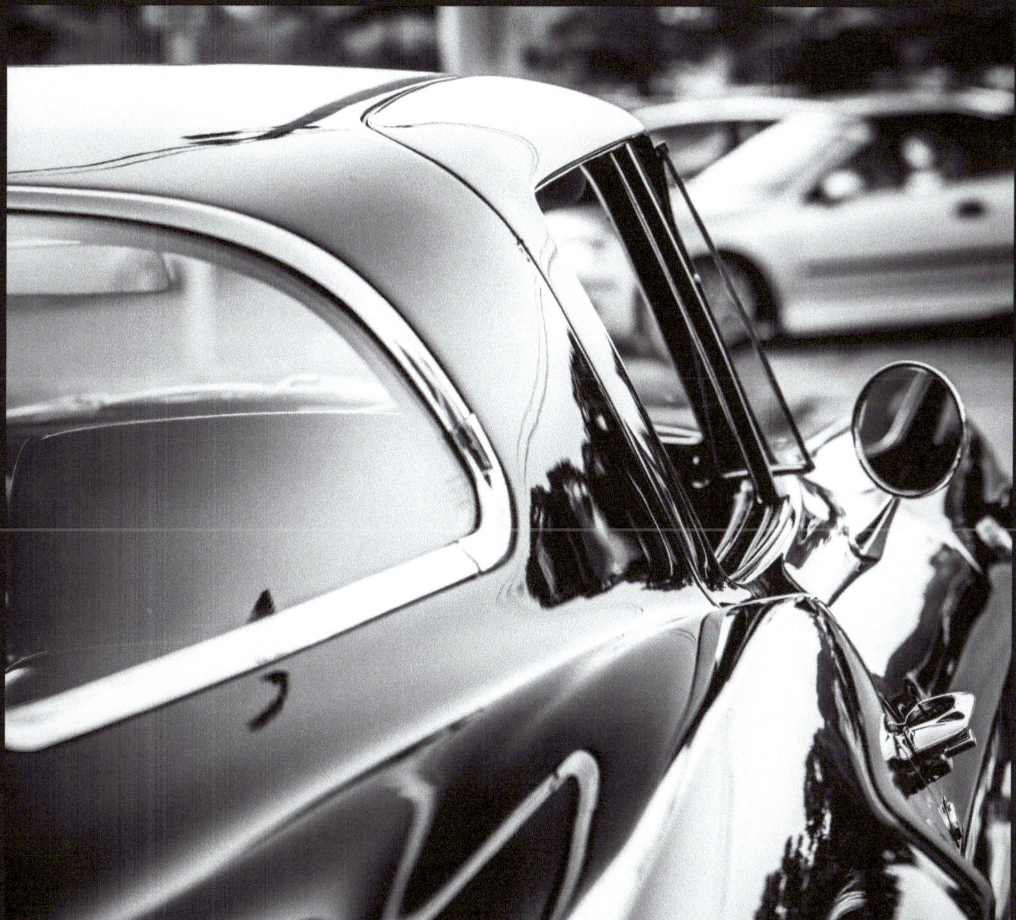

Michael Dubenetsky, Corvette, photograph

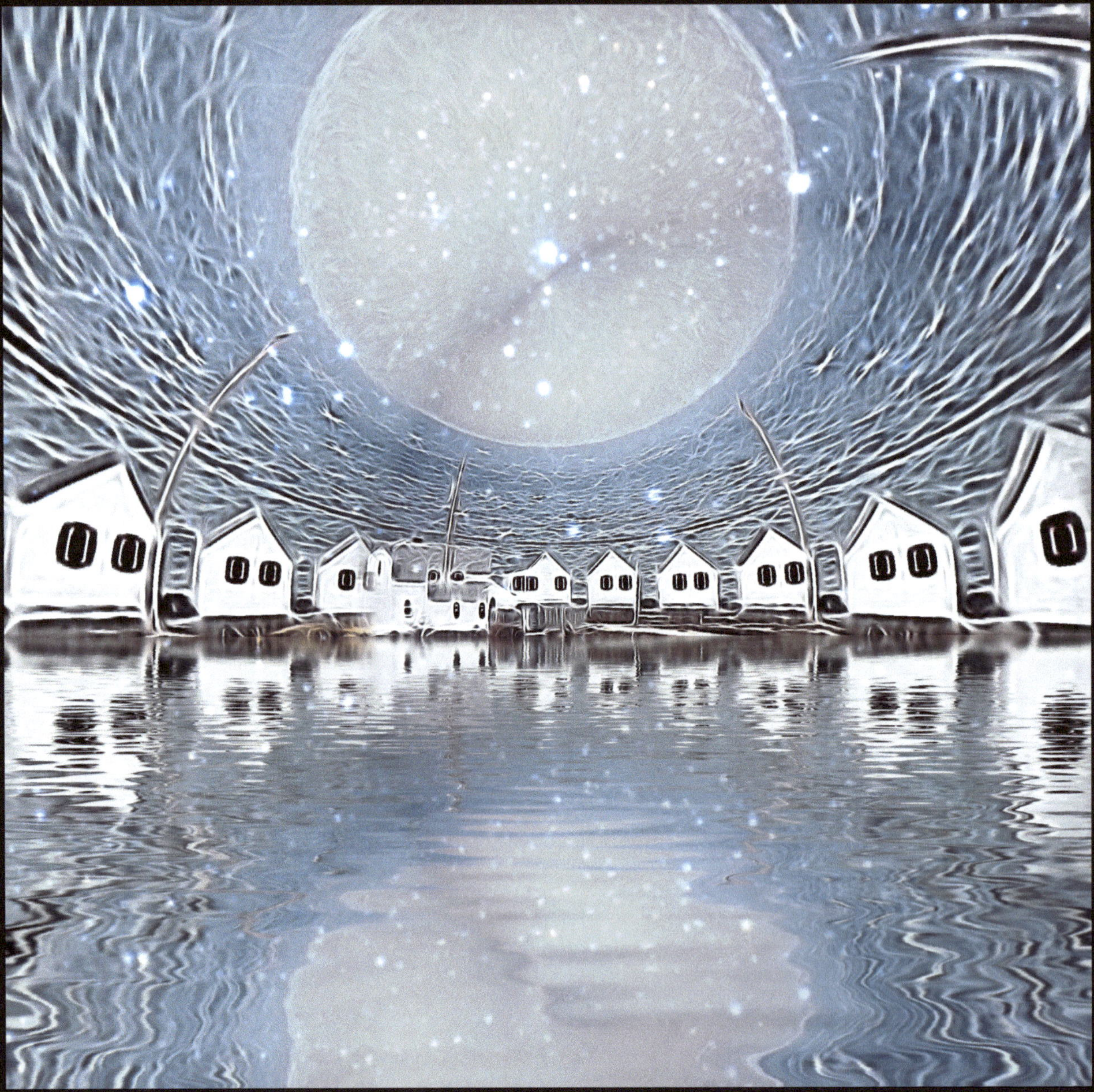

Carol Dunn, Full Moon at the Lake House, altered photograph

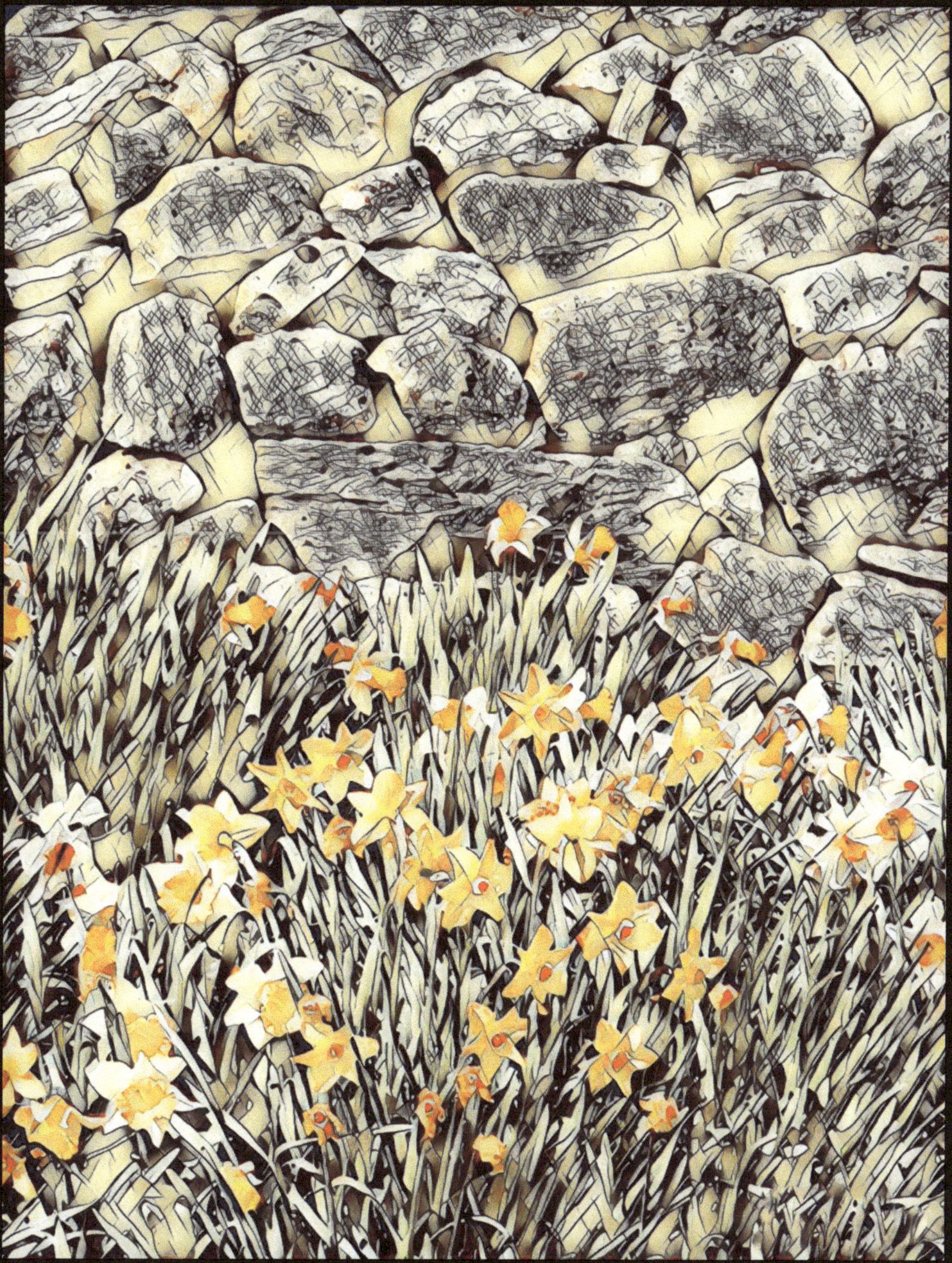

Carol Dunn, Dance of the Daffodils, altered photograph

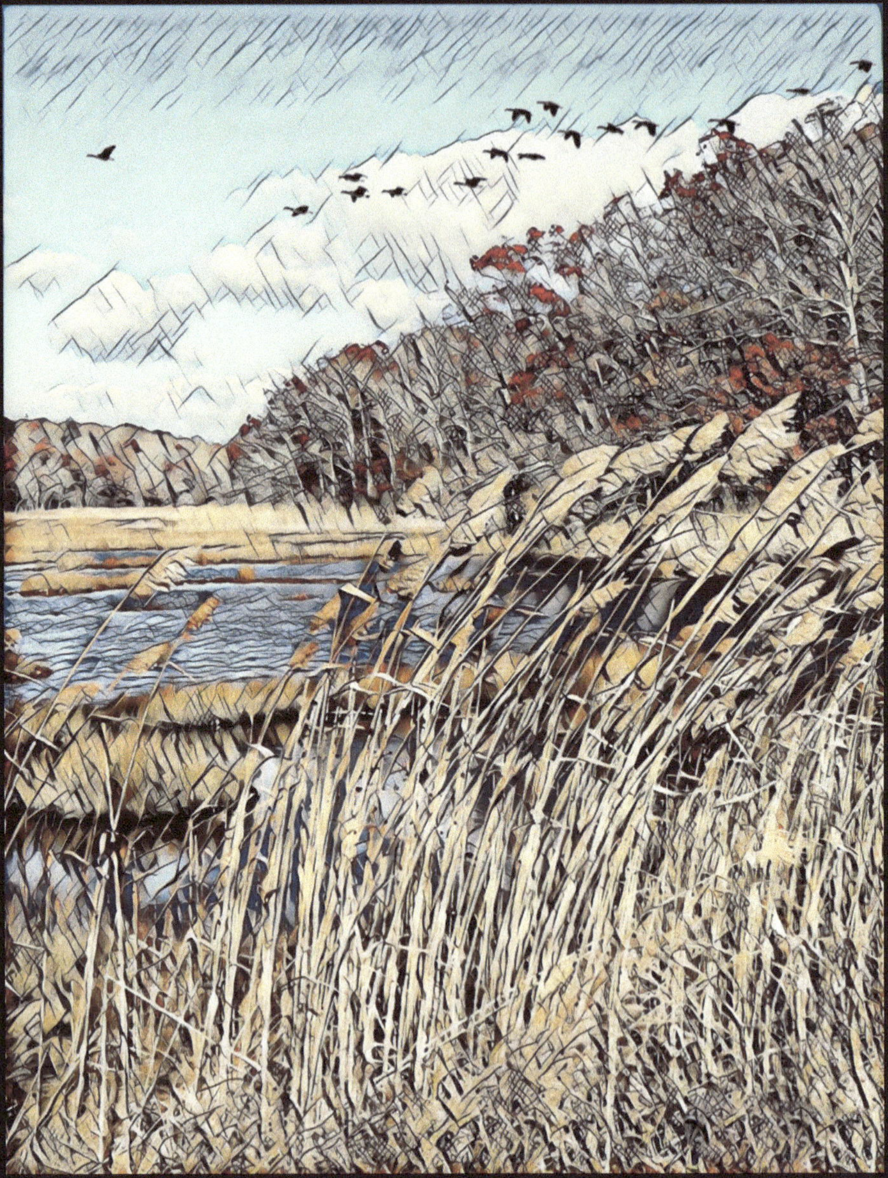

Carol Dunn, Heading South, altered photograph and photo collage

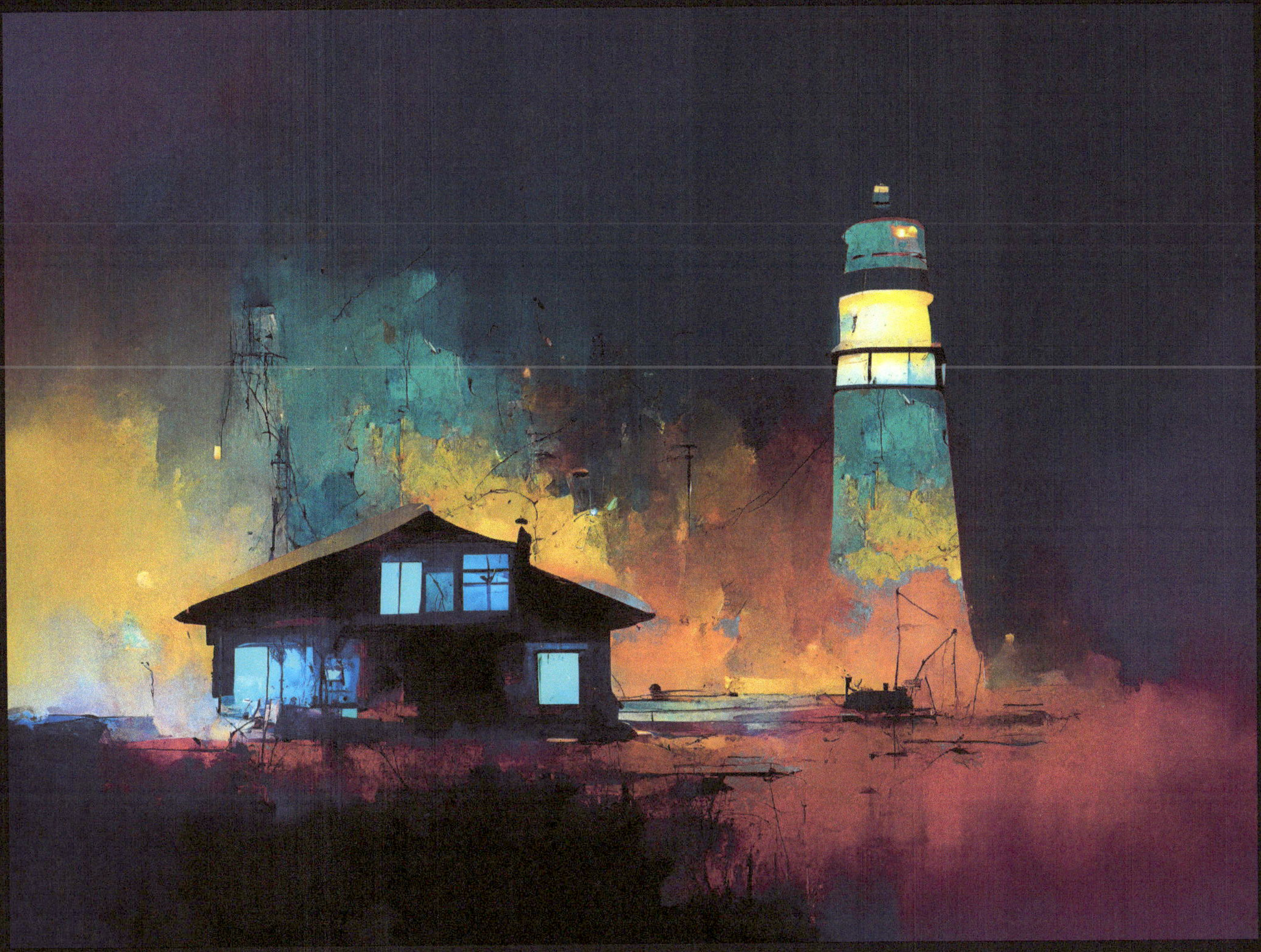

Carol Dunn, Keeper of the Light, photograph altered with AI

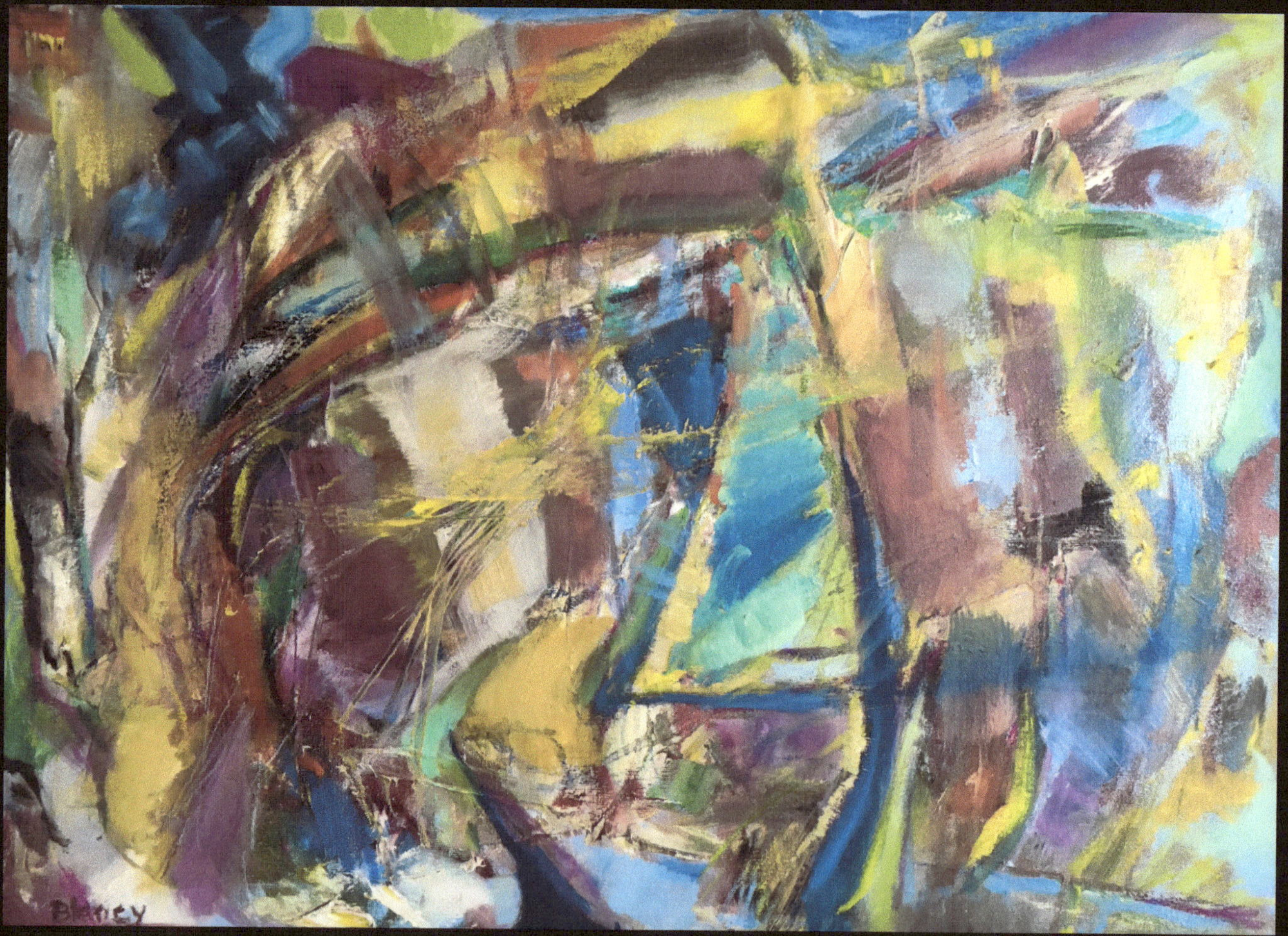

Blaney Harris, Concept 12, oil and pastel on canvas

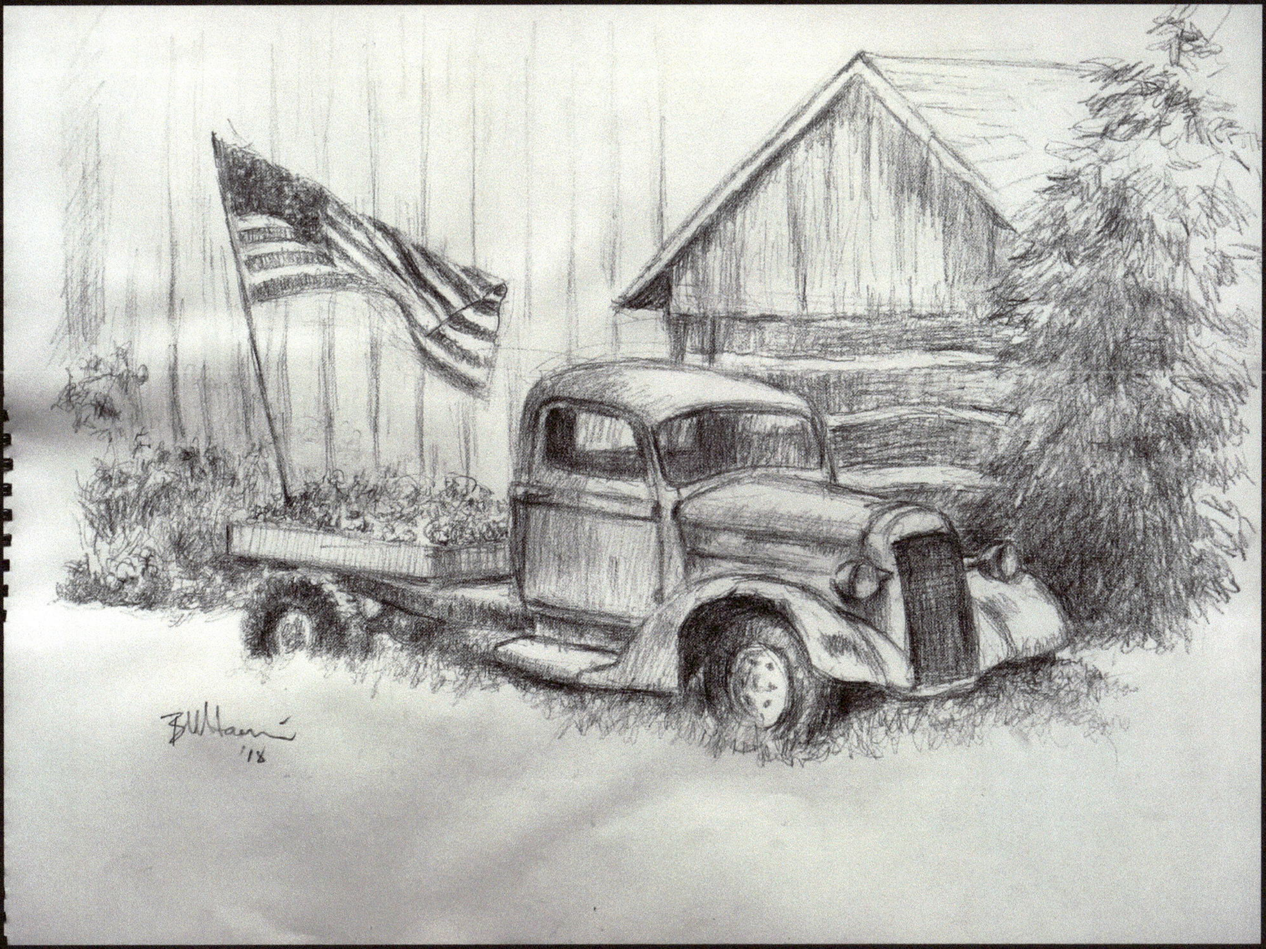

Blaney Harris, The Old Truck, pencil on paper

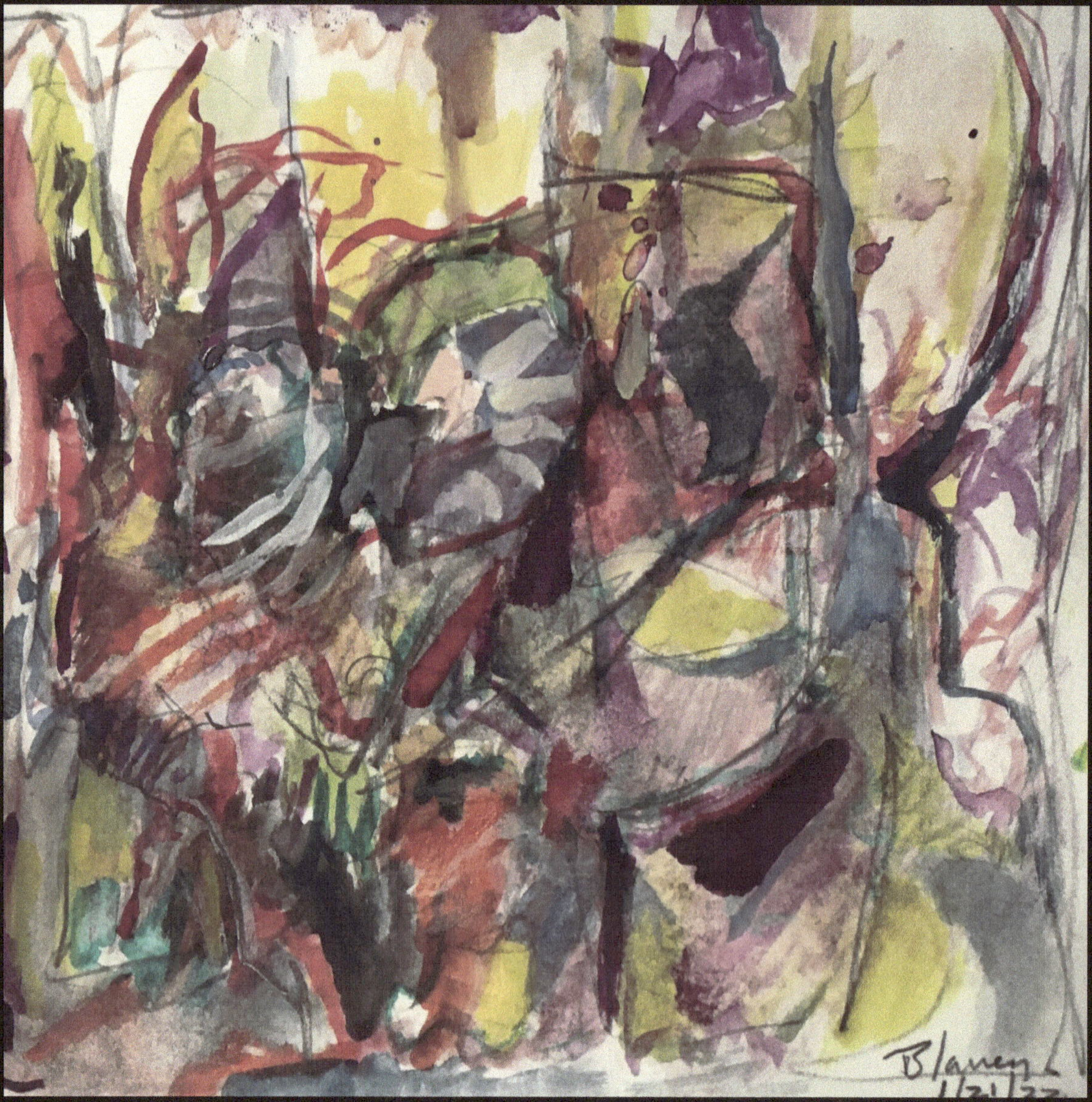

Blaney Harris, The Remains of Autumn, watercolor on paper

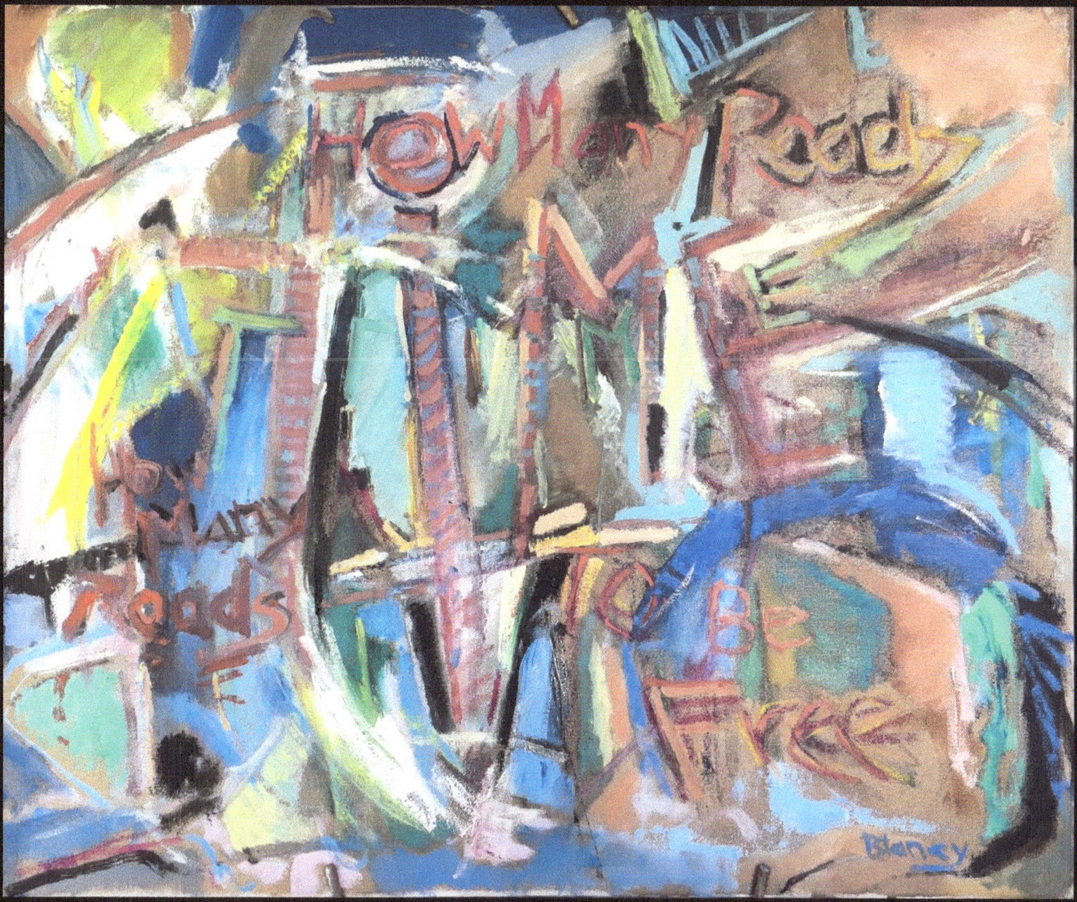

Blaney Harris, How Many Roads, oil and pastel on canvas

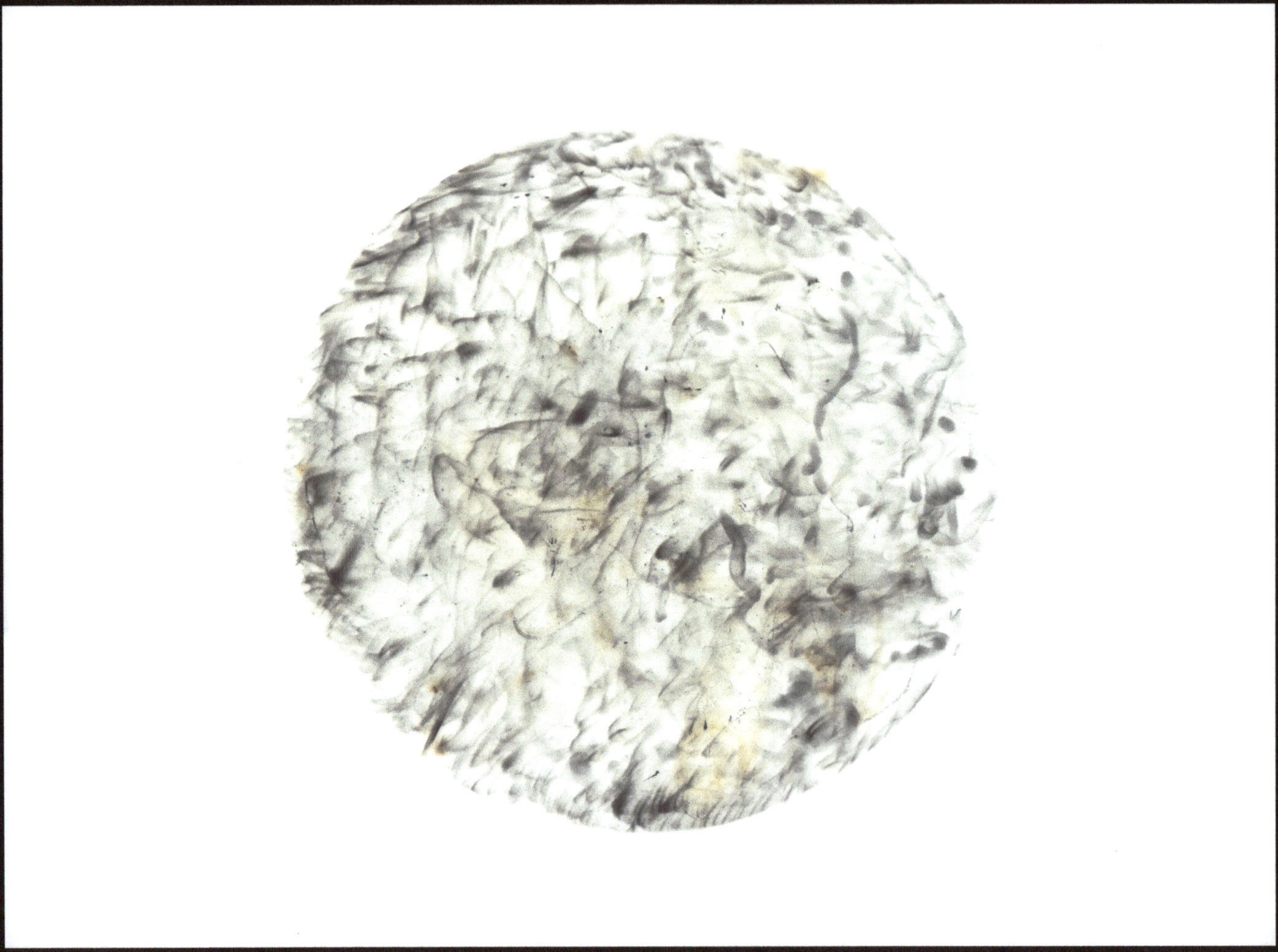

Sandra Jeknavorian, Smoke Breathing Shadows, smoke on canvas

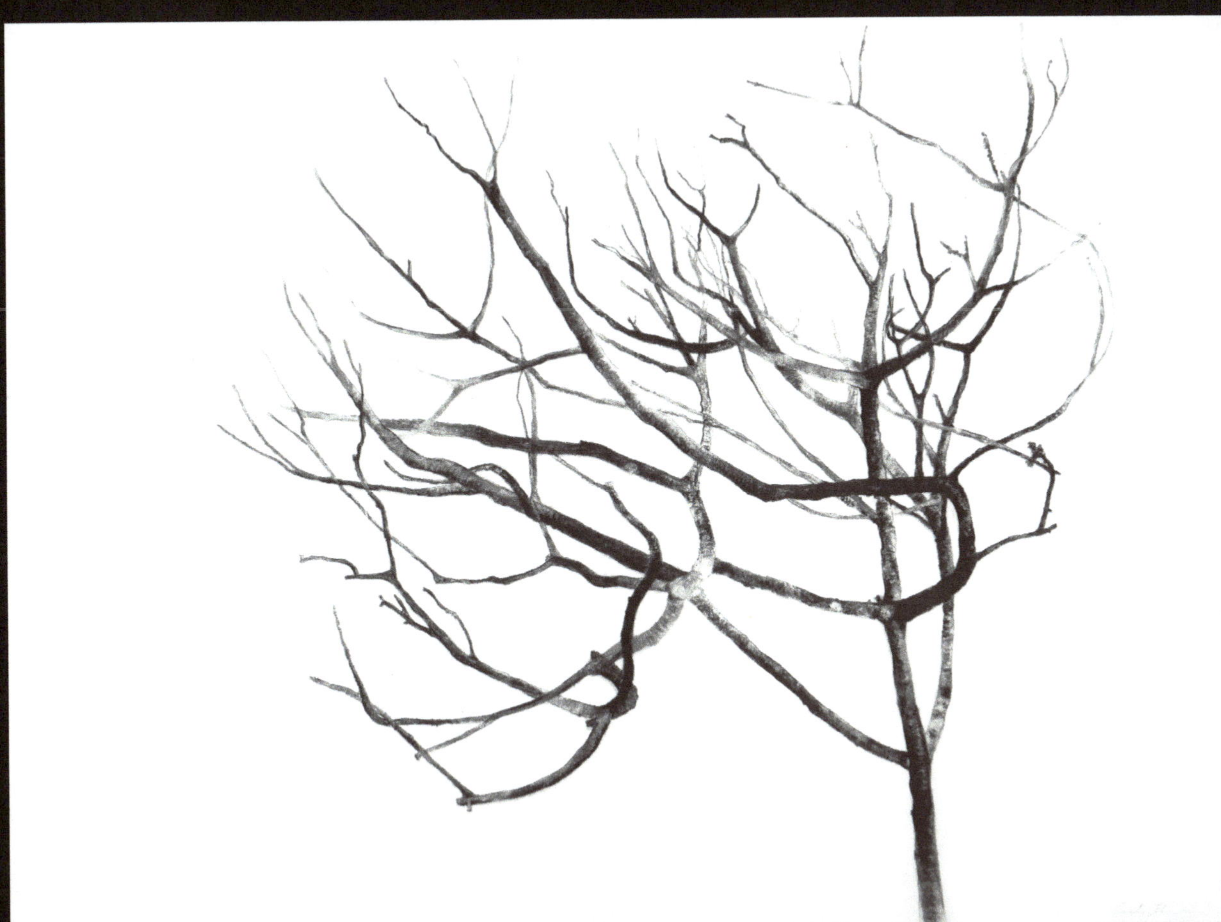

Sandra Jeknavorian, The Breeze Rustles through the Trees,
charcoal on paper

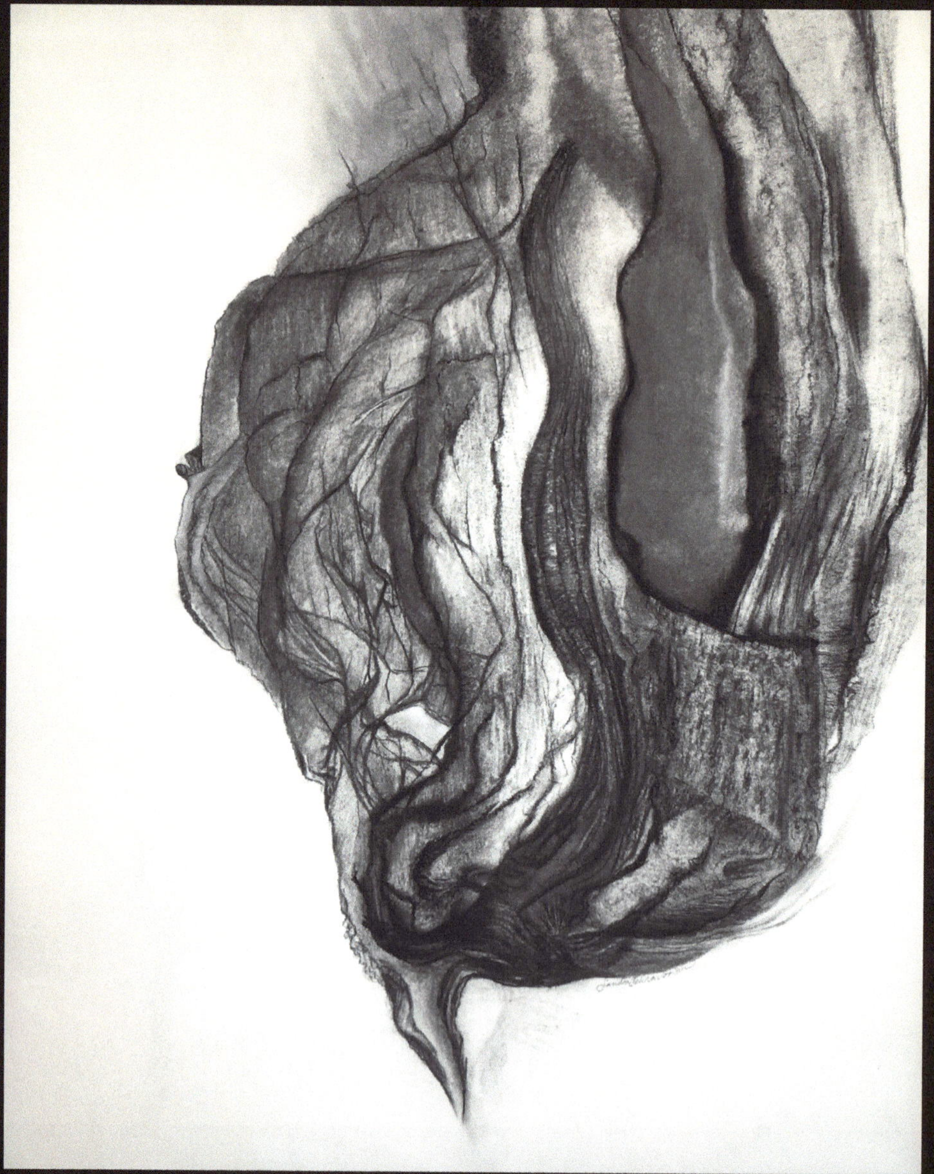

Sandra Jeknavorian, Everything and Nothing, charcoal and pastel on paper

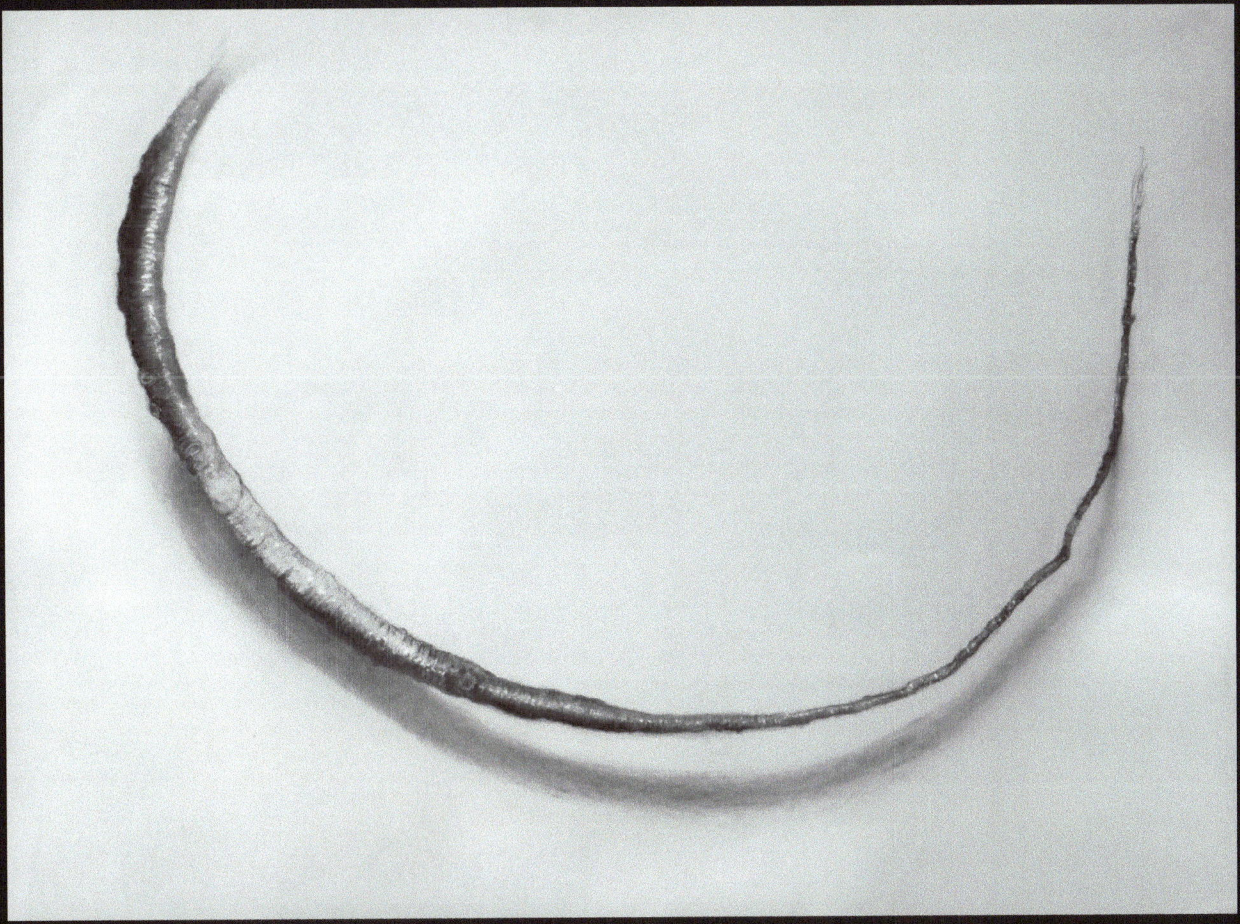

Sandra Jeknavorian, Tree Hoop, charcoal and pastel on paper

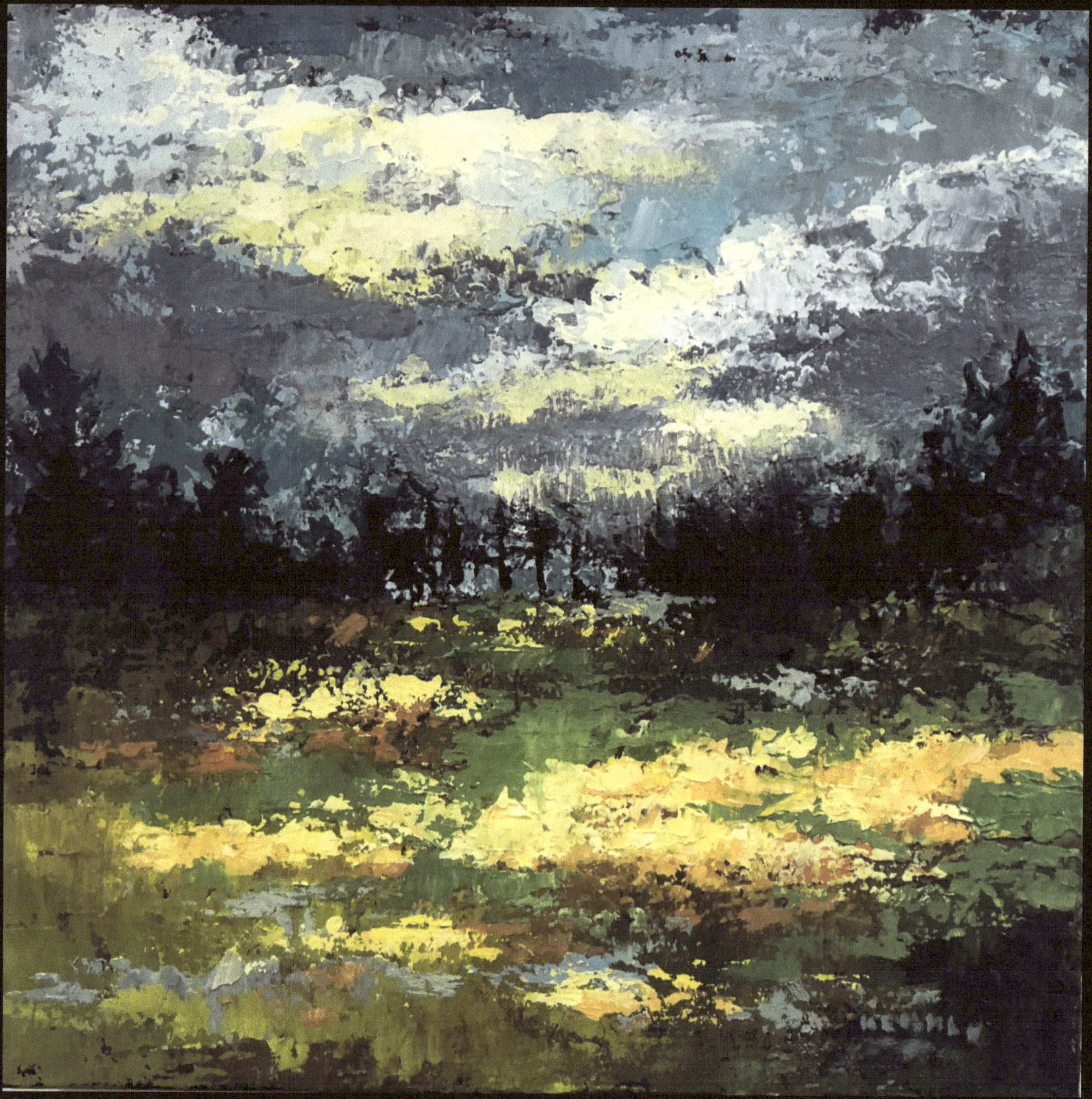

Susan Scott Kenney, After the Storm, acrylic on canvas

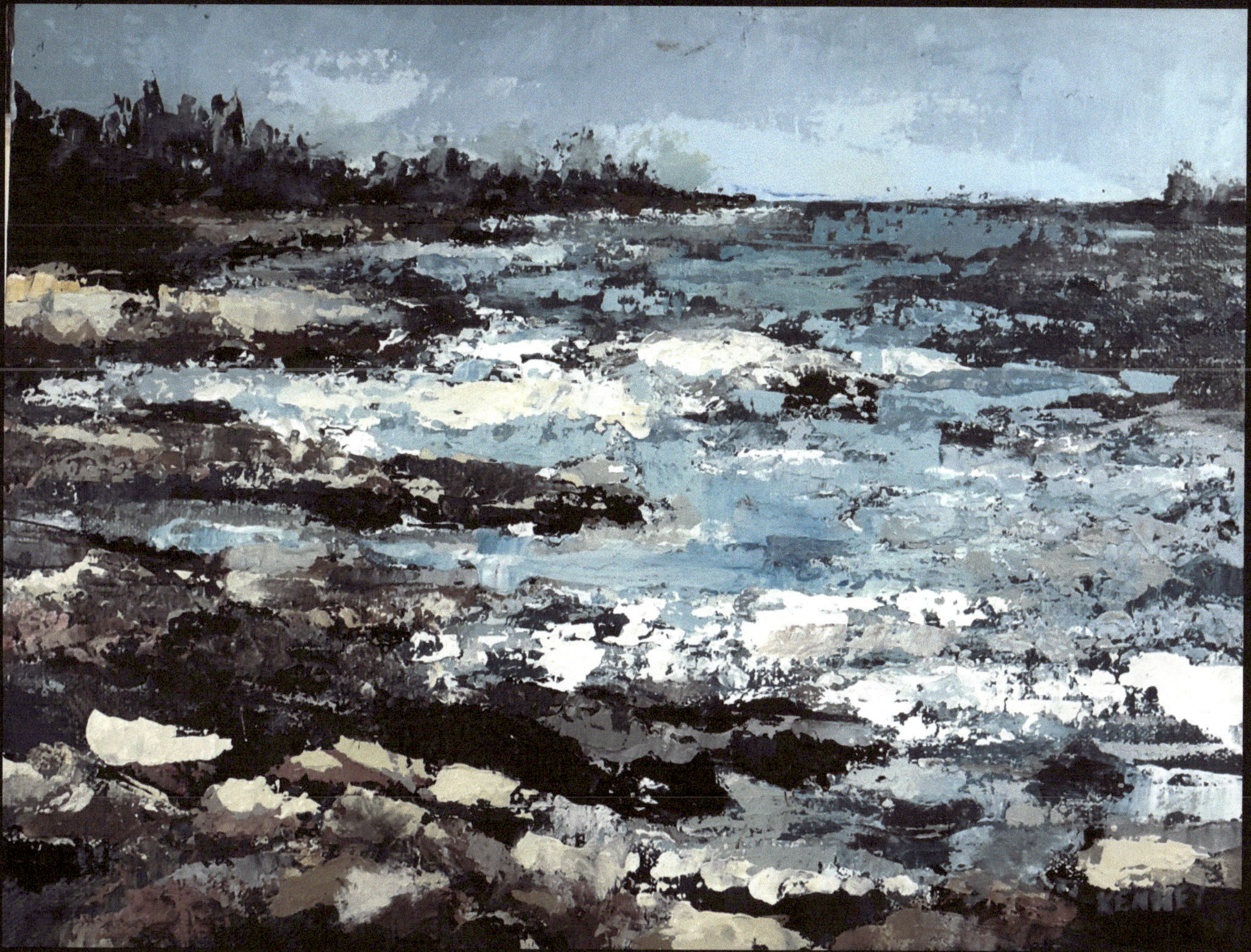

Susan Scott Kenney, Maine Shoreline, acrylic on canvas

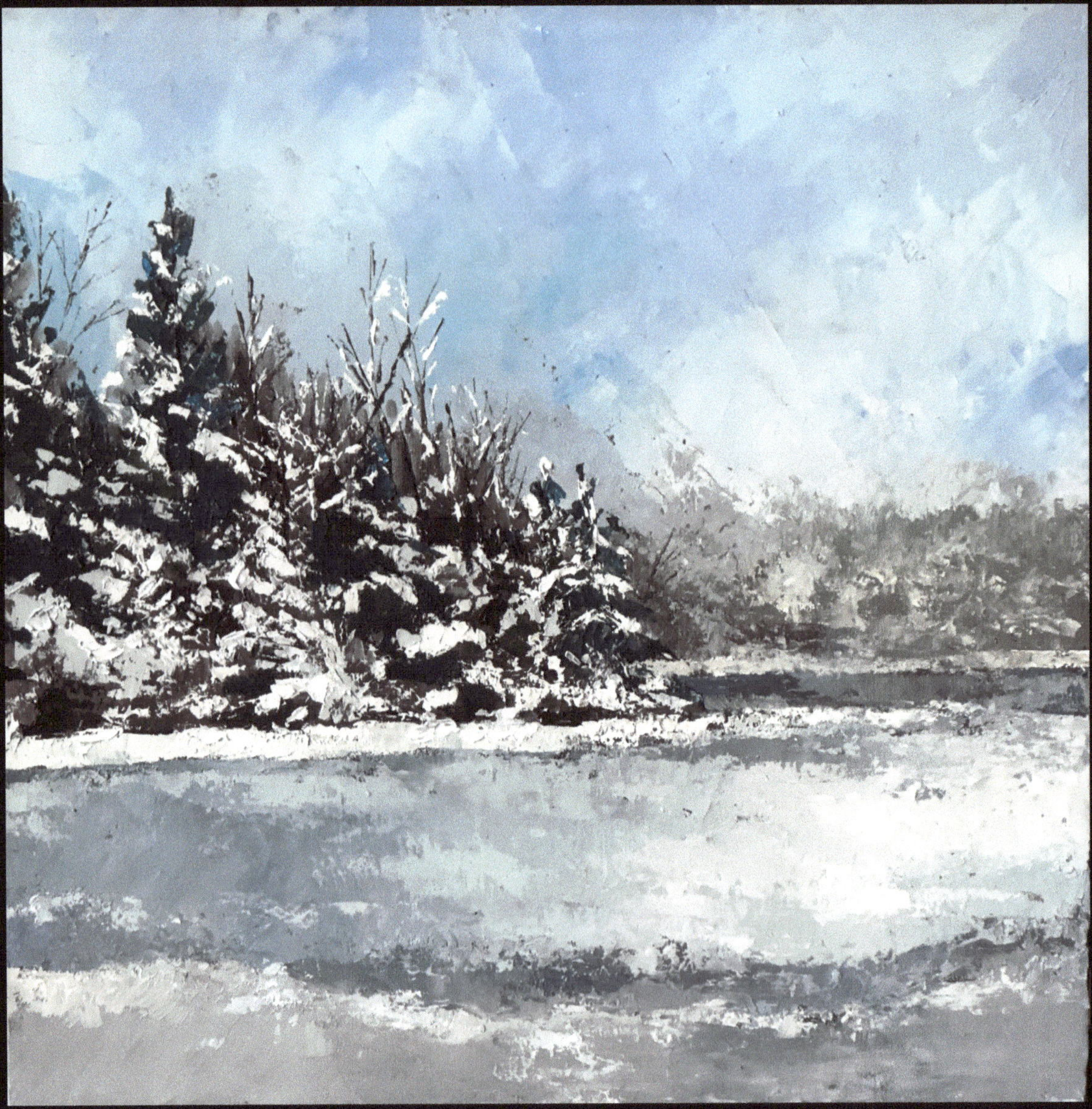

Susan Scott Kenney, Winter Frosting, acrylic on canvas

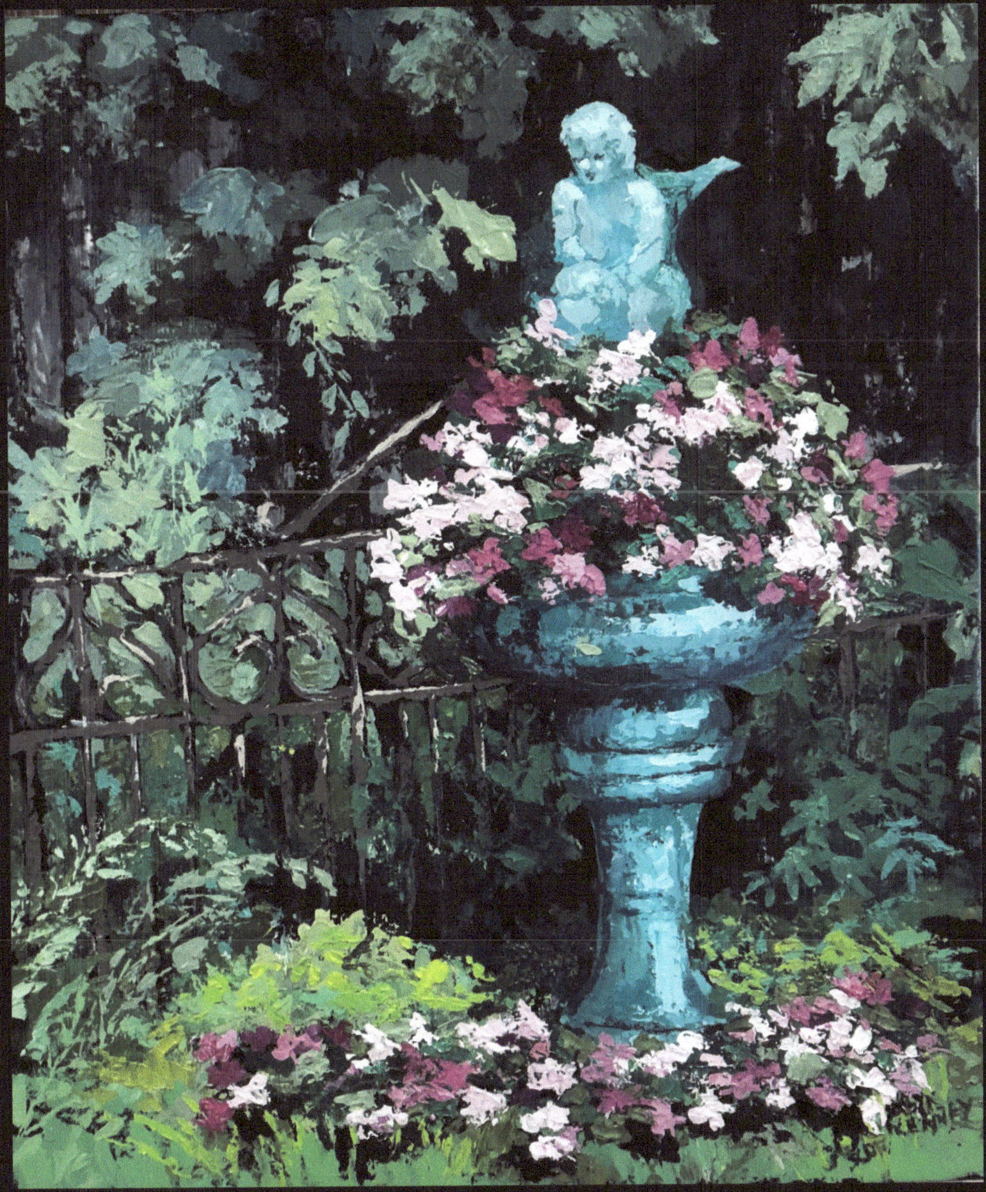

Susan Scott Kenney, Angel in the Garden, acrylic on canvas

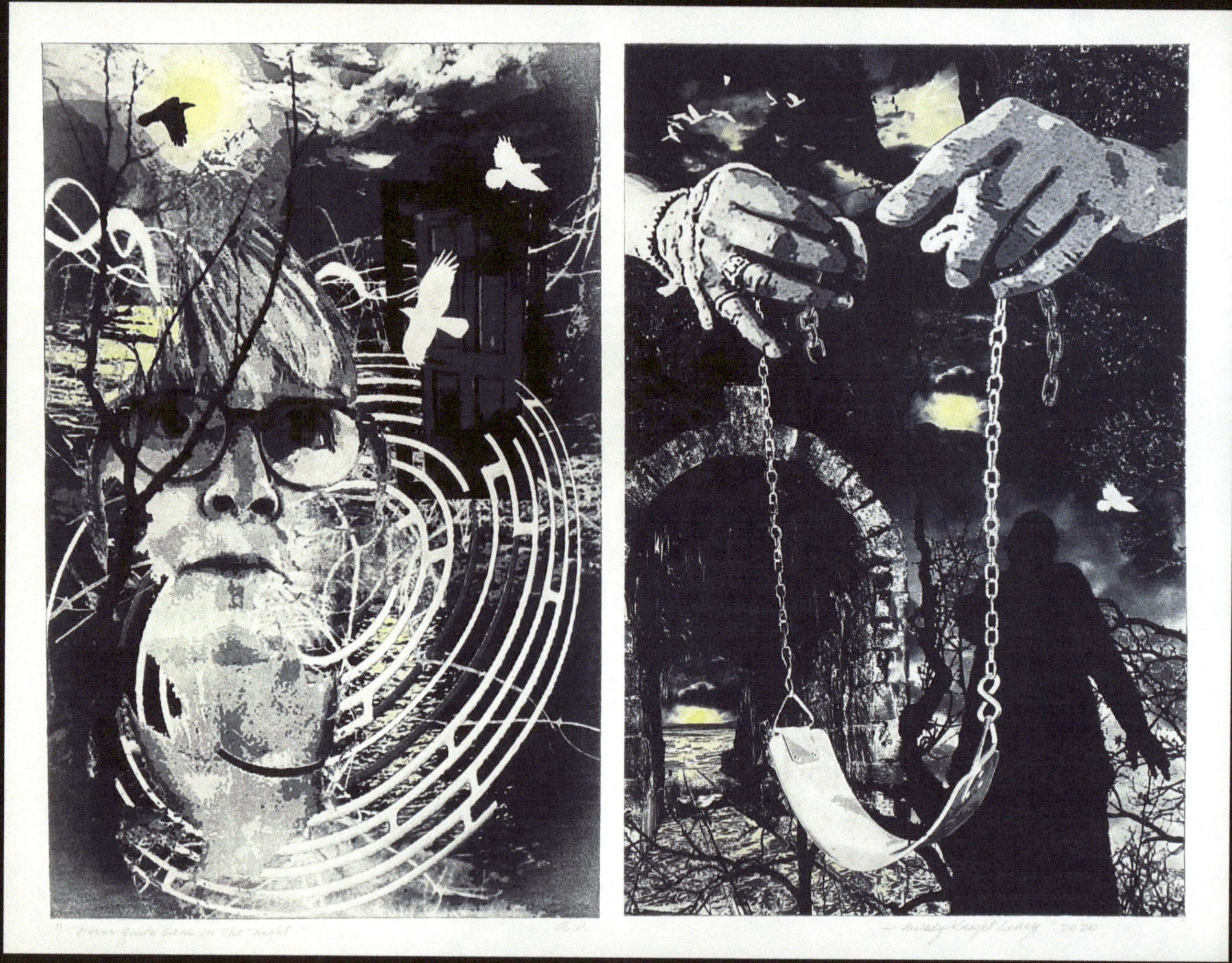

Melody Knight Leary, Mysteries of the Night,
photopolymer intaglio print with watercolor

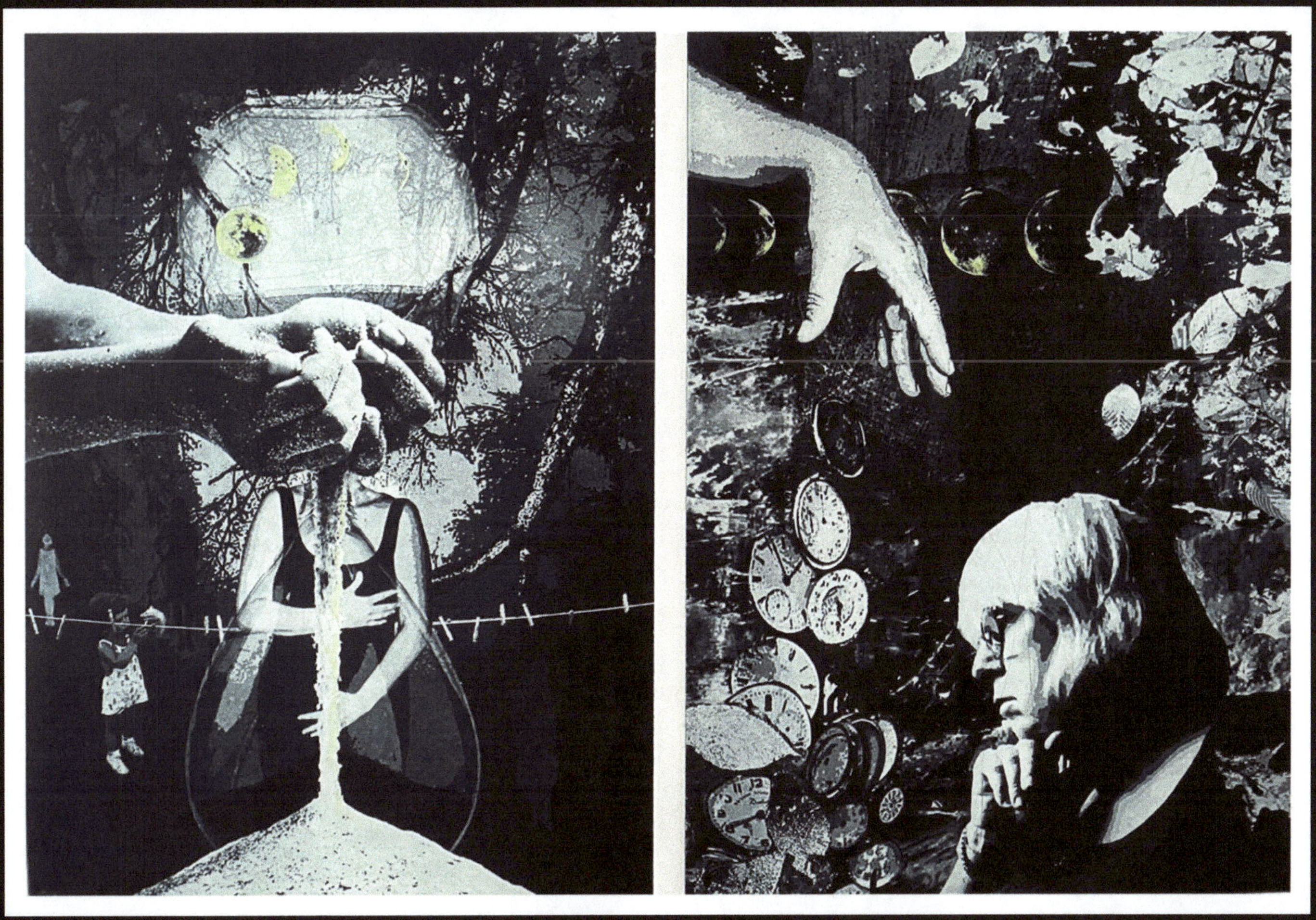

Melody Knight Leary, Melancholy,
photopolymer intaglio print with watercolor

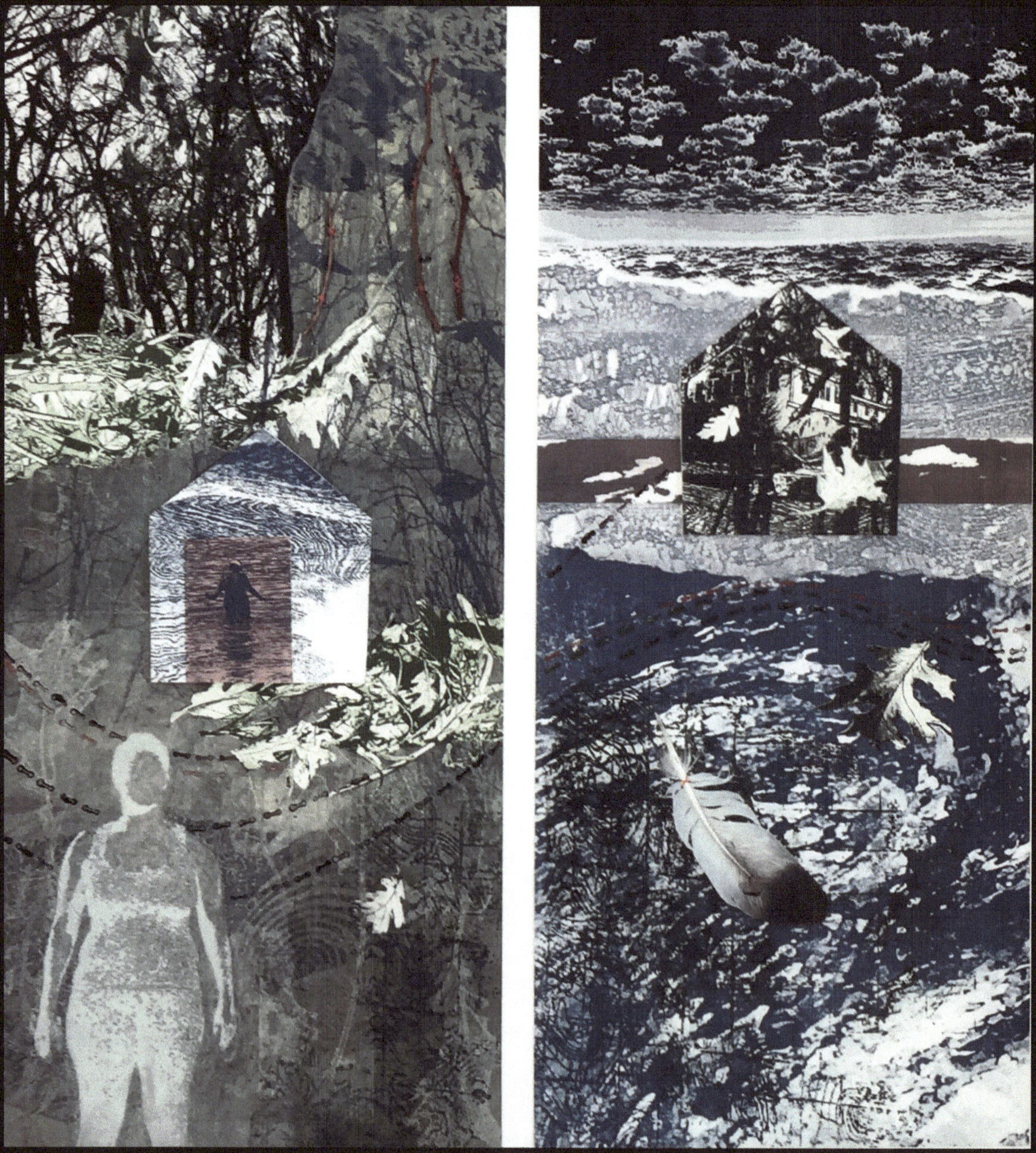

Melody Knight Leary, Conundrum: Woods or Water?,
photopolymer intaglio print with watercolor

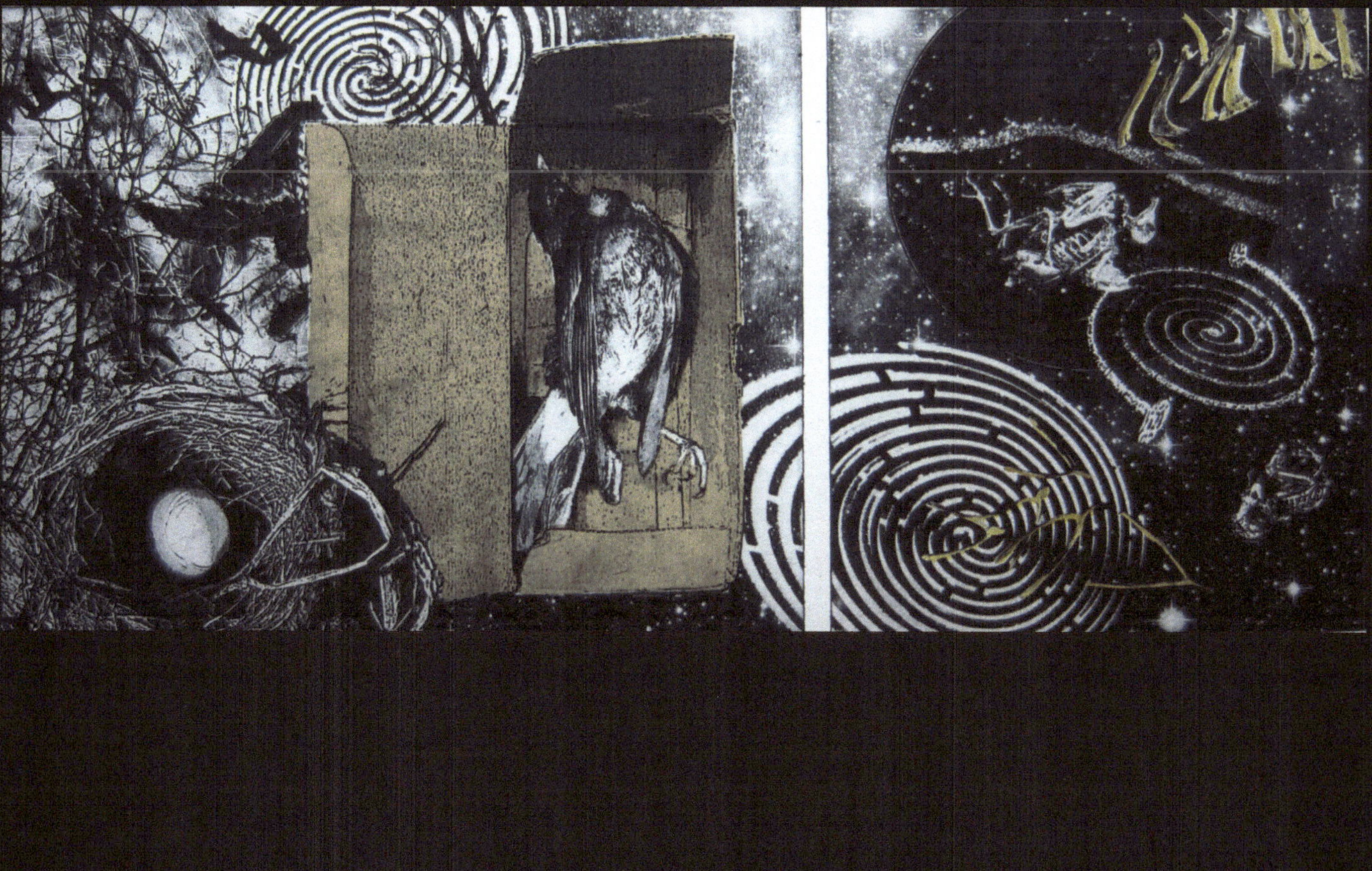

Melody Knight Leary, From Here to God,
photopolymer intaglio print with chine collé

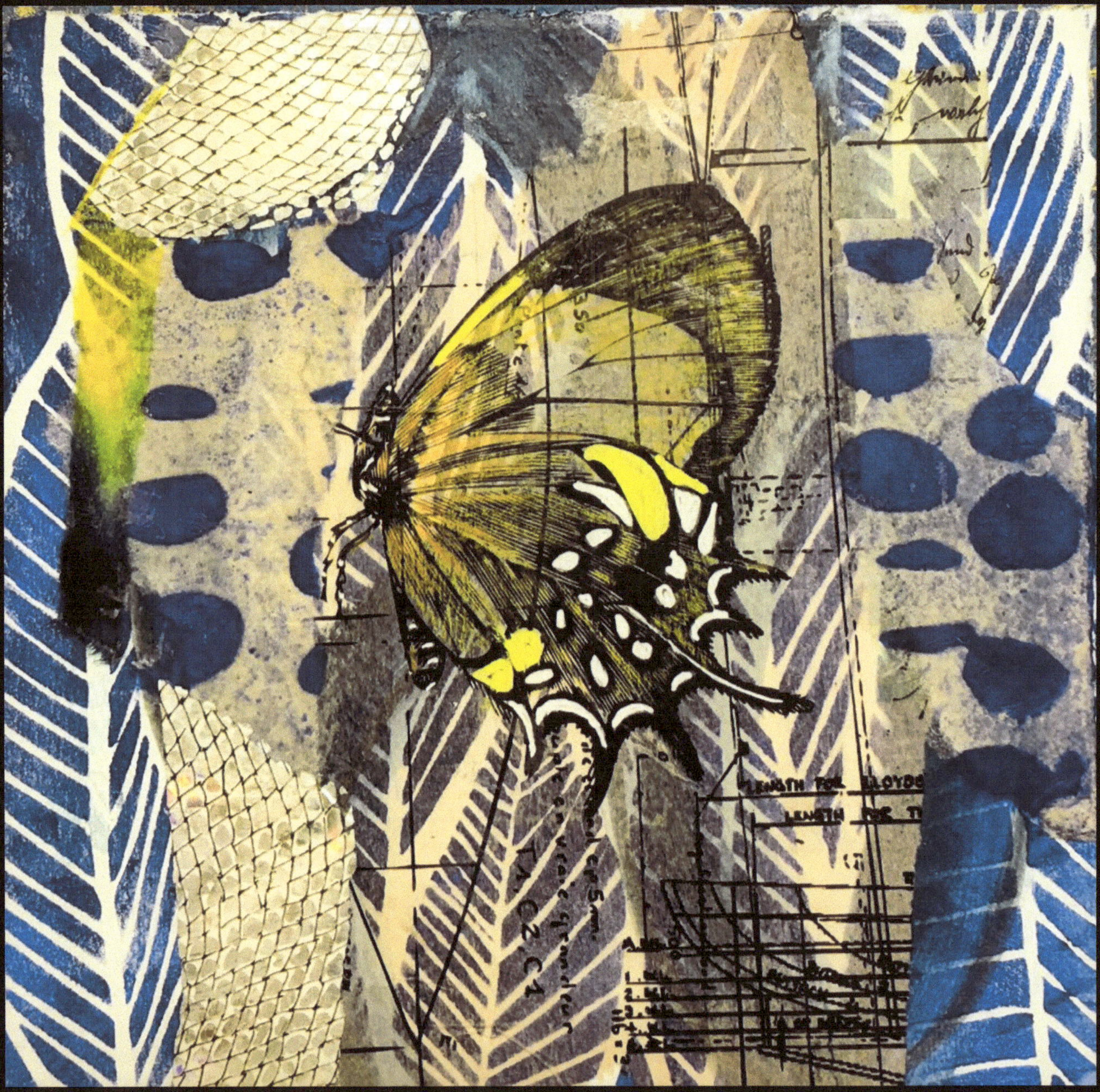

Gerlinde Lehner, Butterfly Fun, acrylic

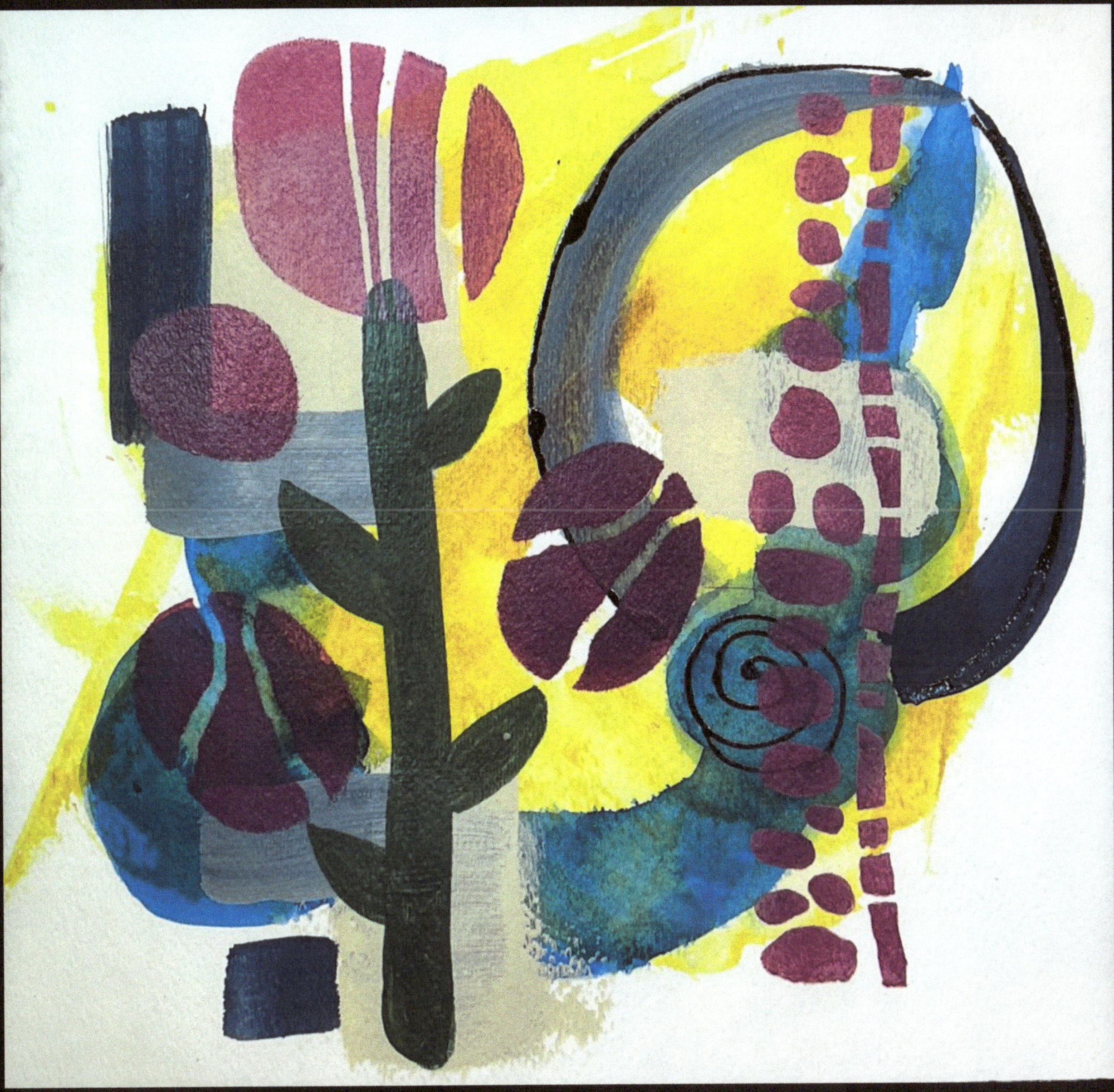

Gerlinde Lehner, Garden of Flowers, acrylic

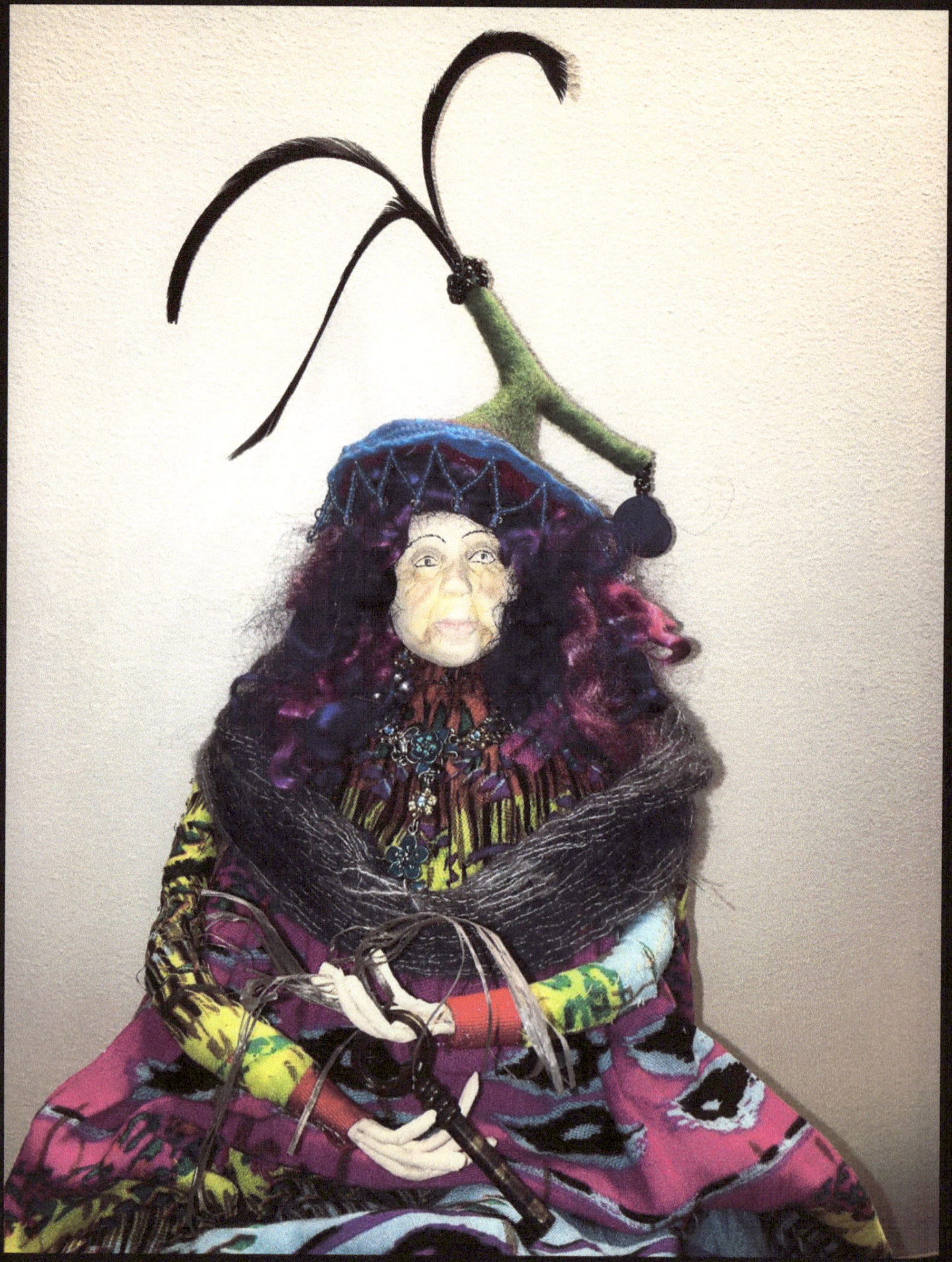

Gerlinde Lehner, The Guardian, handmade doll

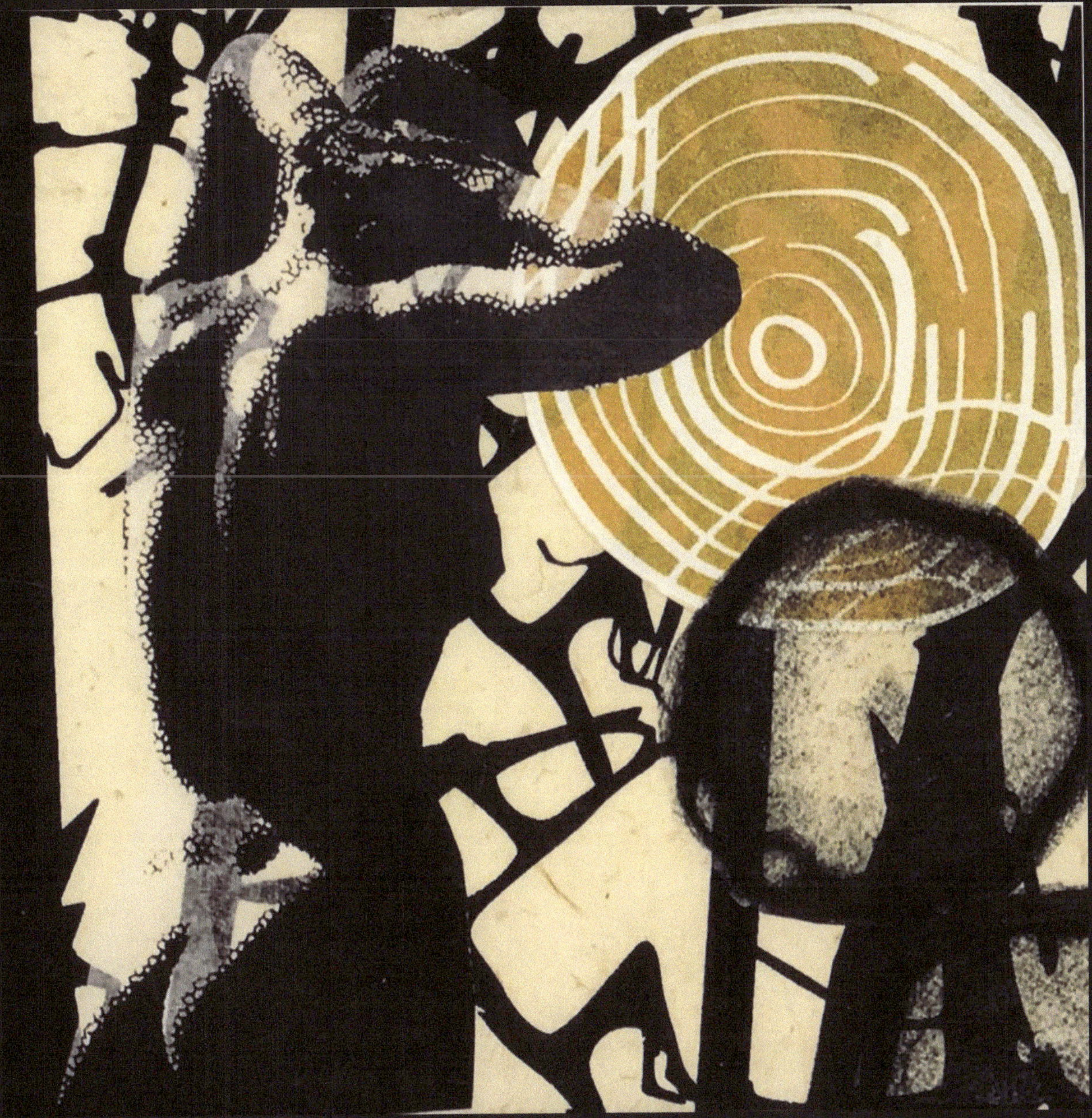

Gerlinde Lehner, Woman in the Woods, collage

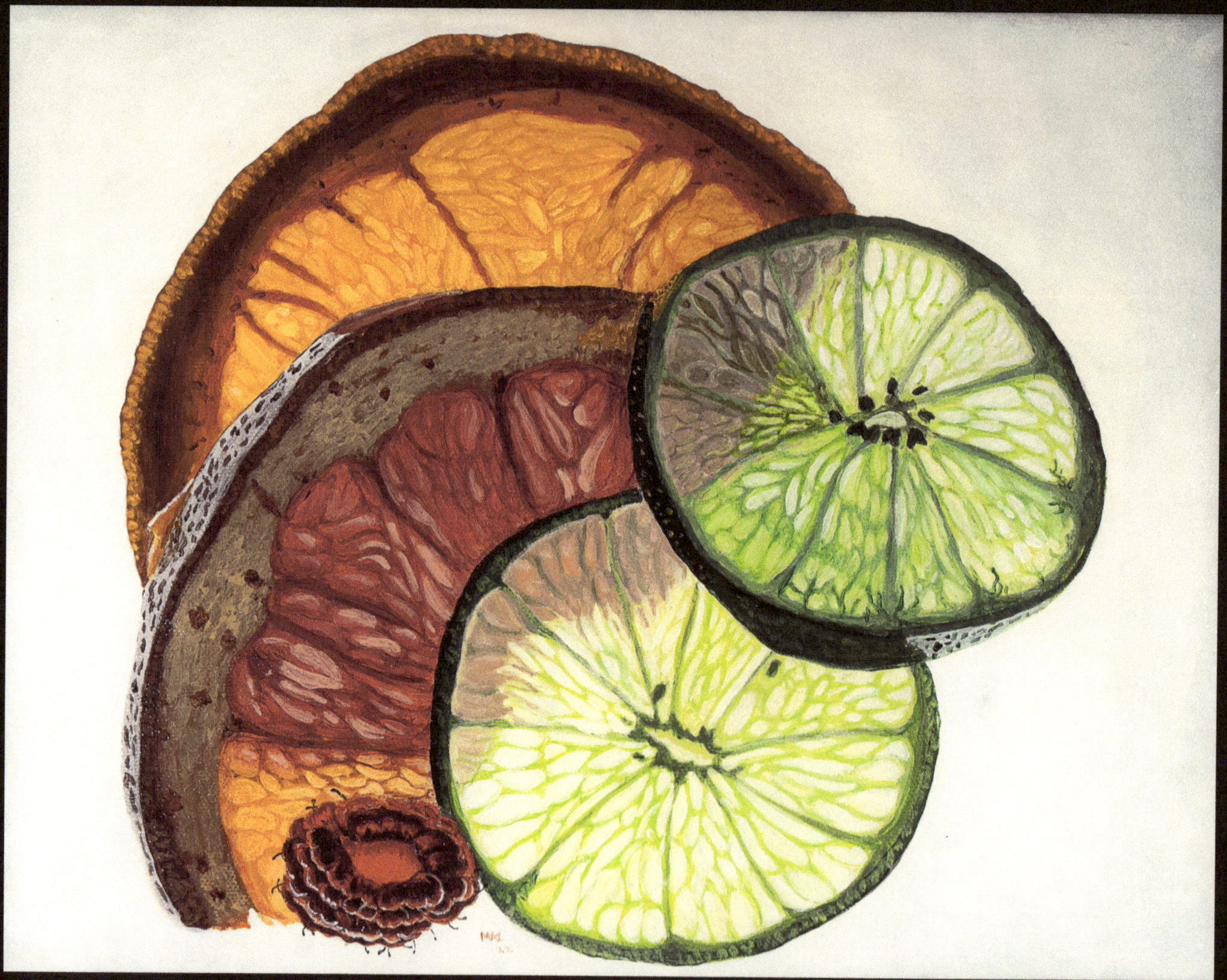

Mary Ann Lewis, Citrus Salad, acrylic on canvas

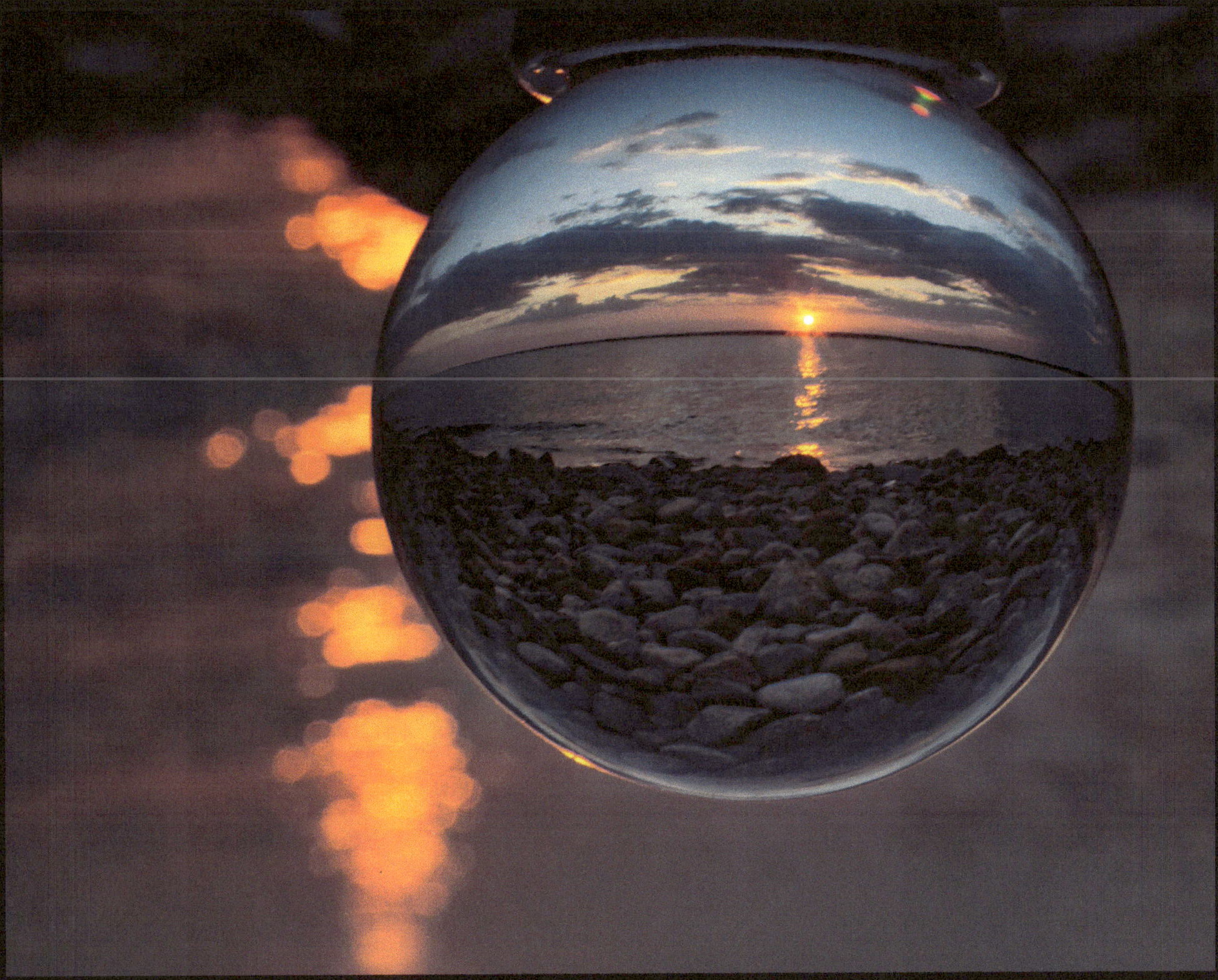

Mary Ann Lewis, Crystal Sunset, ditigal photograph

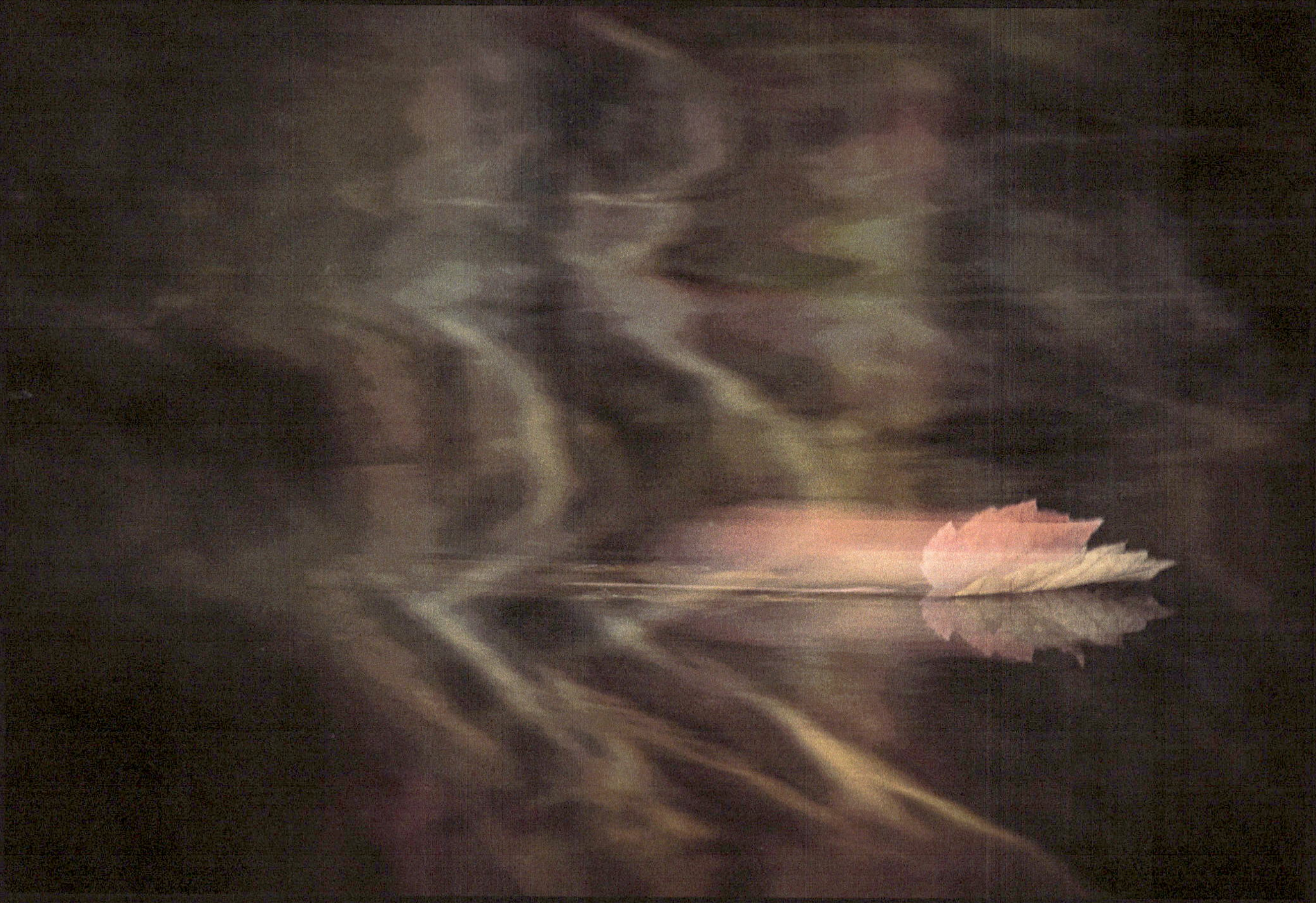

Mary Ann Lewis, Like an Arrow, digital photograph

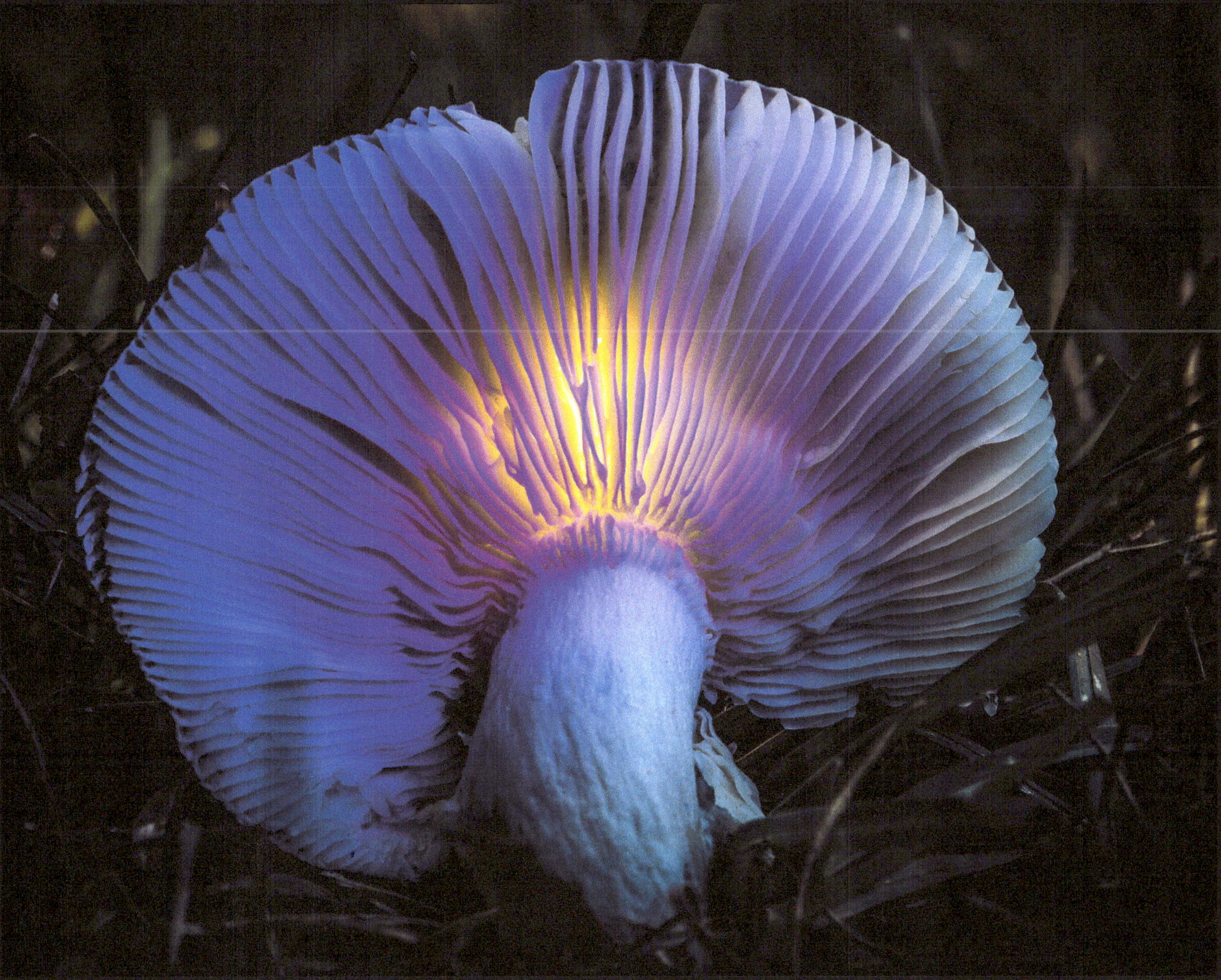

Mary Ann Lewis, Magic Mushroom, digital photograph

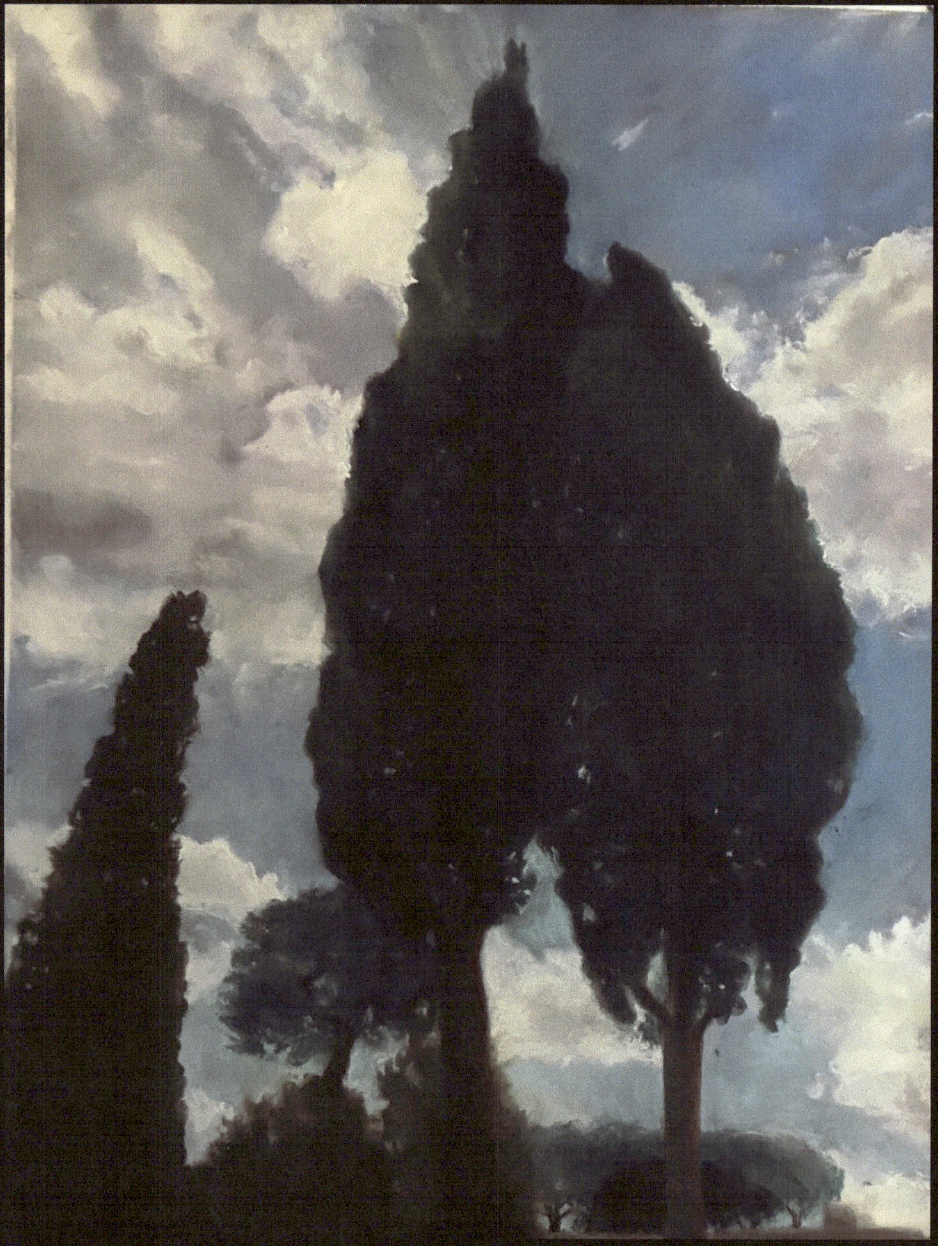

Gabe Lipman, The Forum, pastel on paper

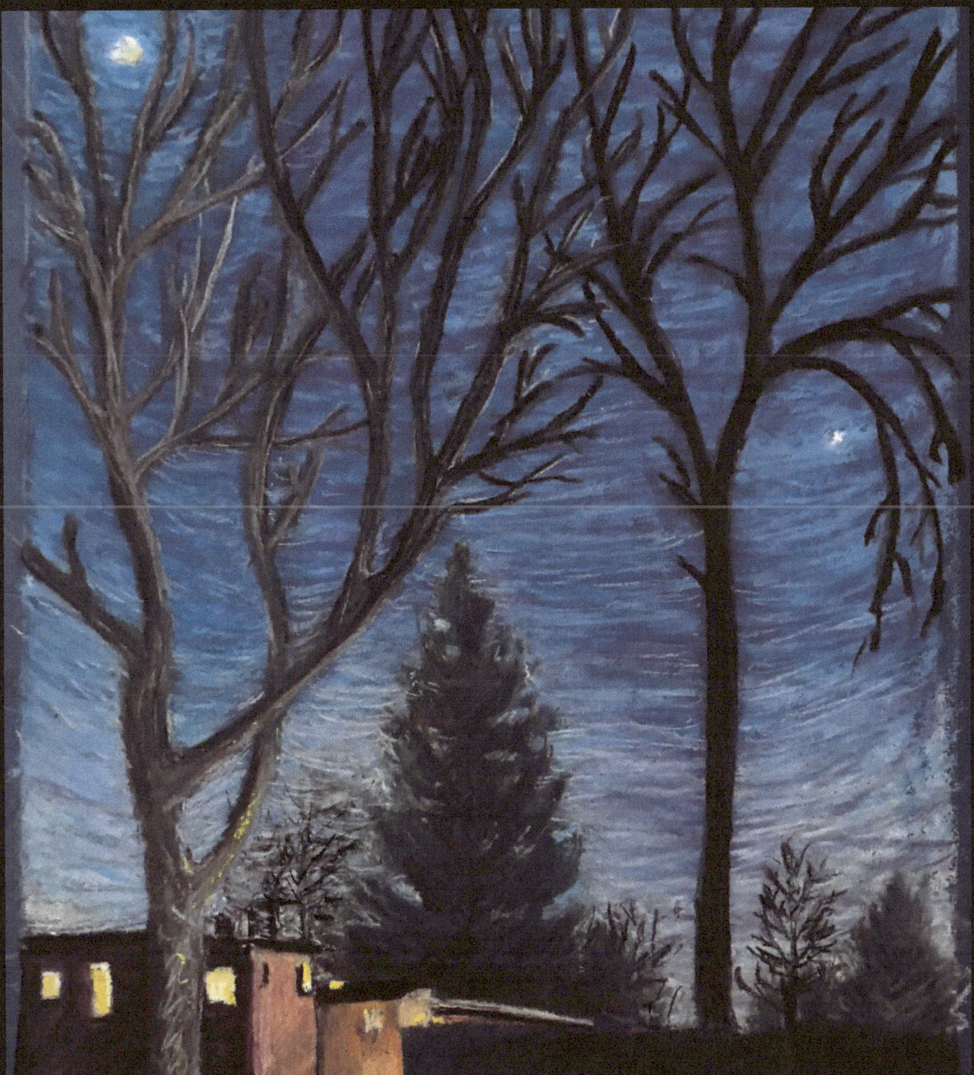

Gabe Lipman, Backyard Views II, pastel on paper

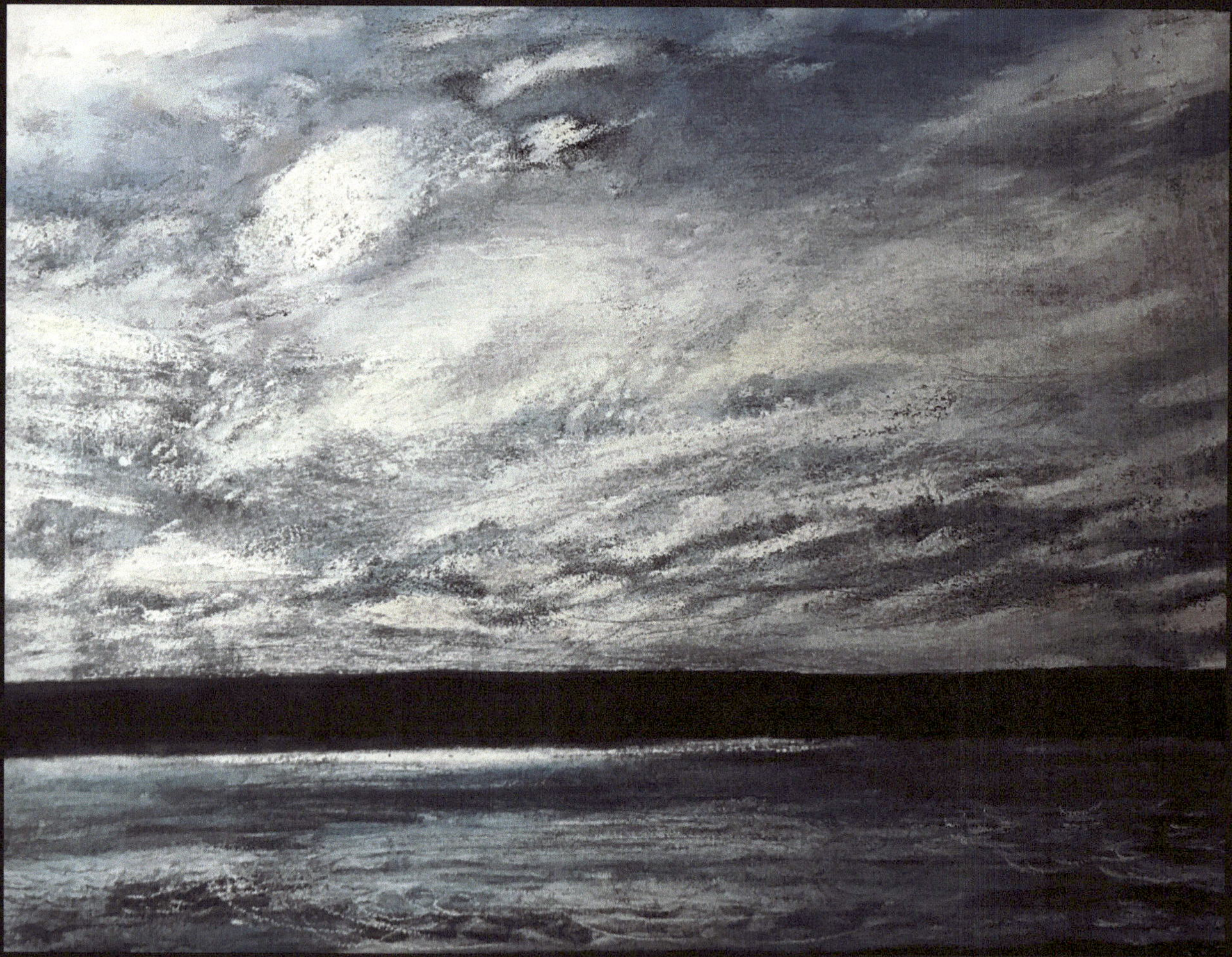

Gabe Lipman, Somewhere in the Bay of Fundy, pastel on paper

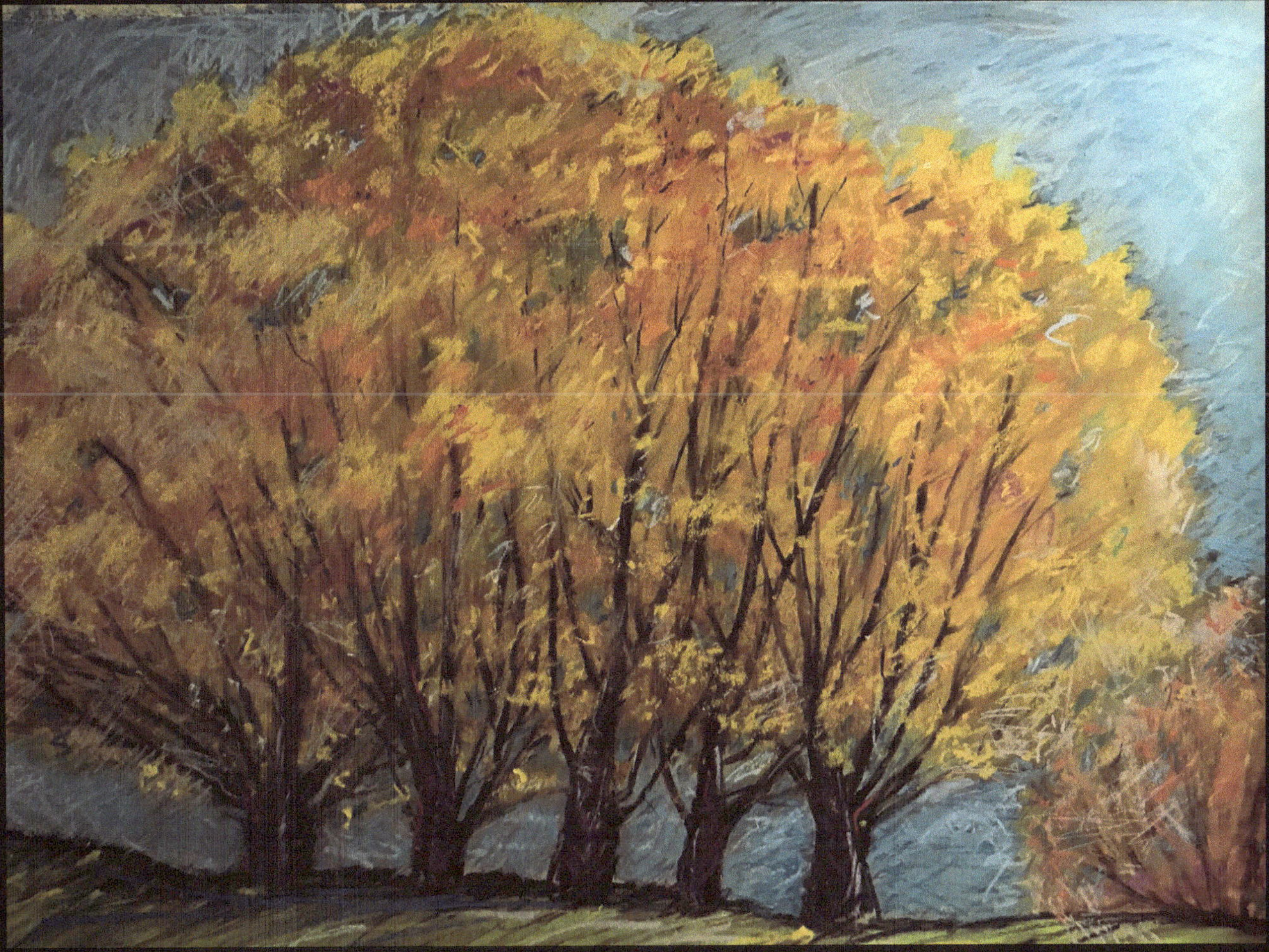

Gabe Lipman, Somewhere in Pennsylvania, pastel on paper

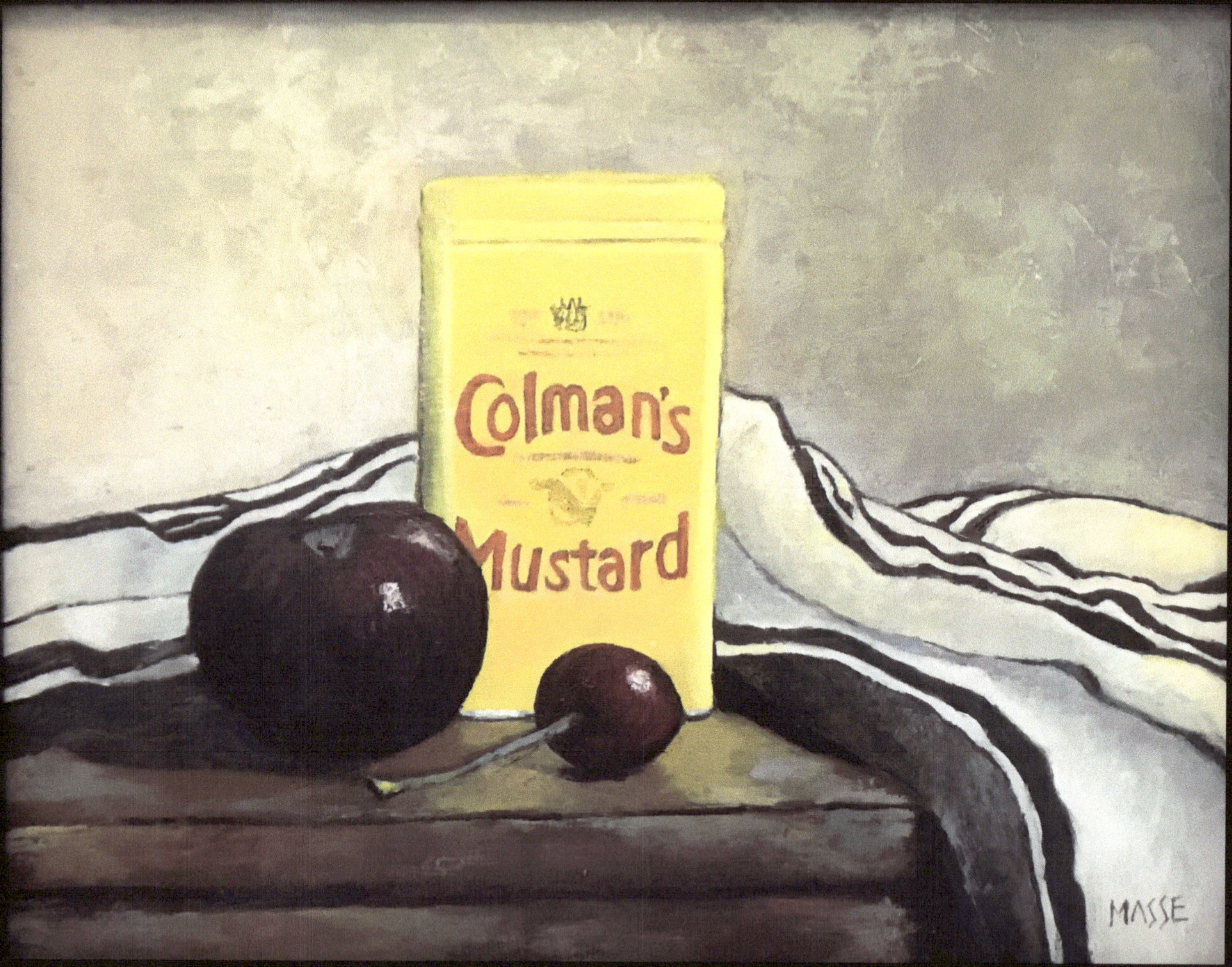

Susan Masse, Coleman's Mustard, oil on canvas

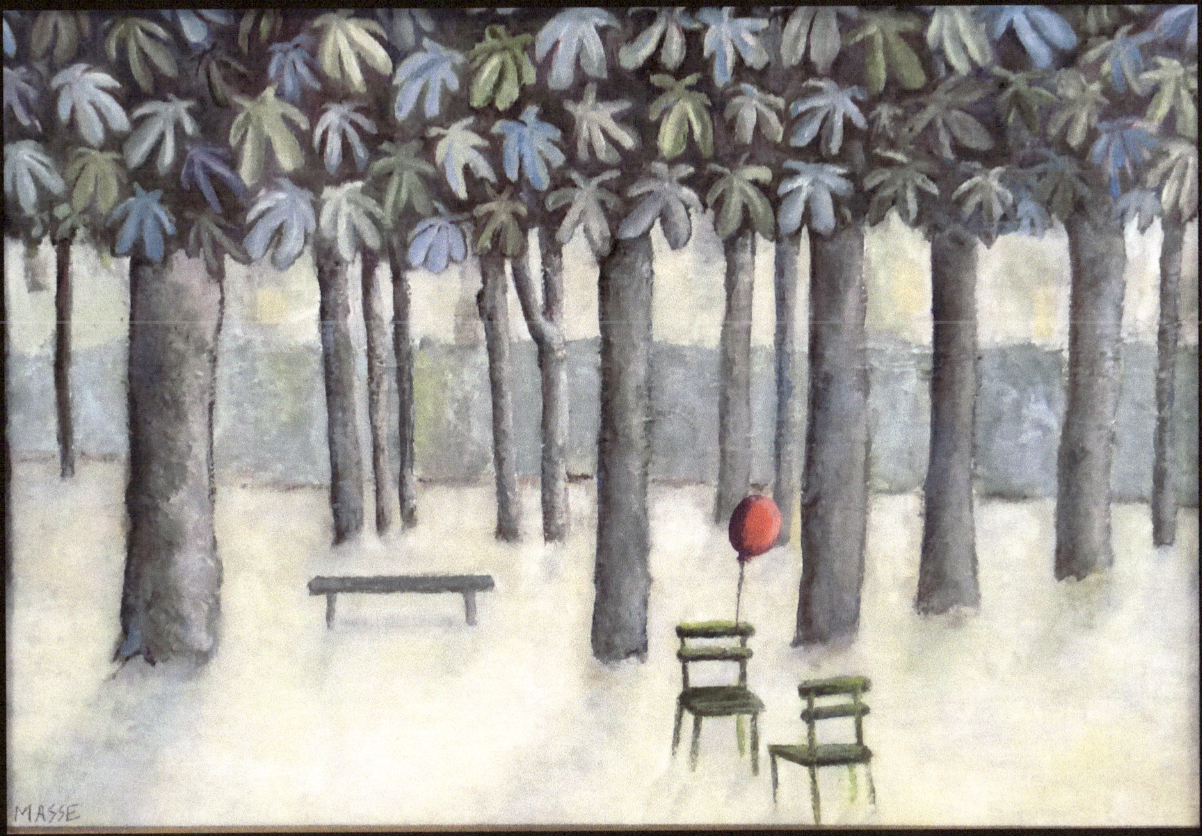

Susan Masse, Paris Tuileries, oil on canvas

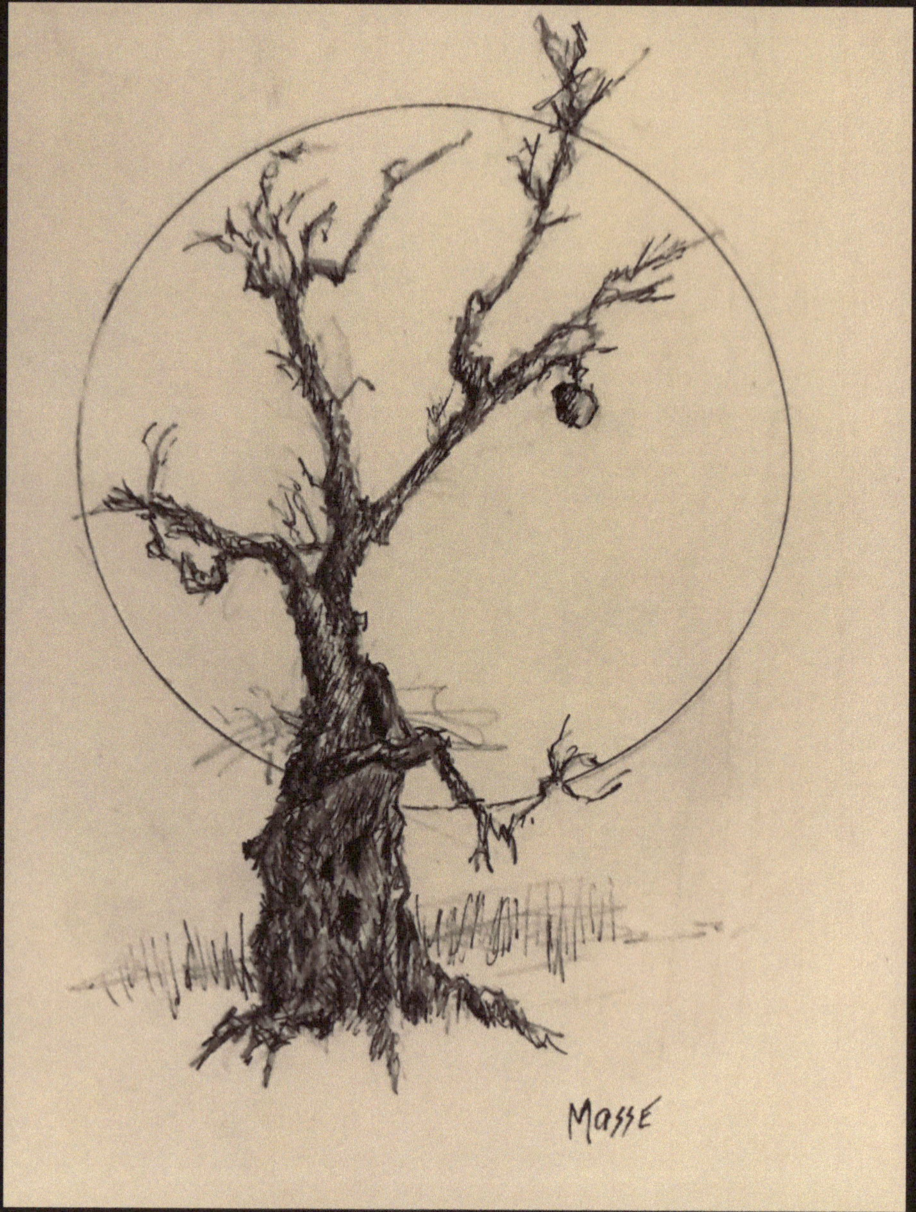

Susan Masse, Egon's Apple, pencil on paper

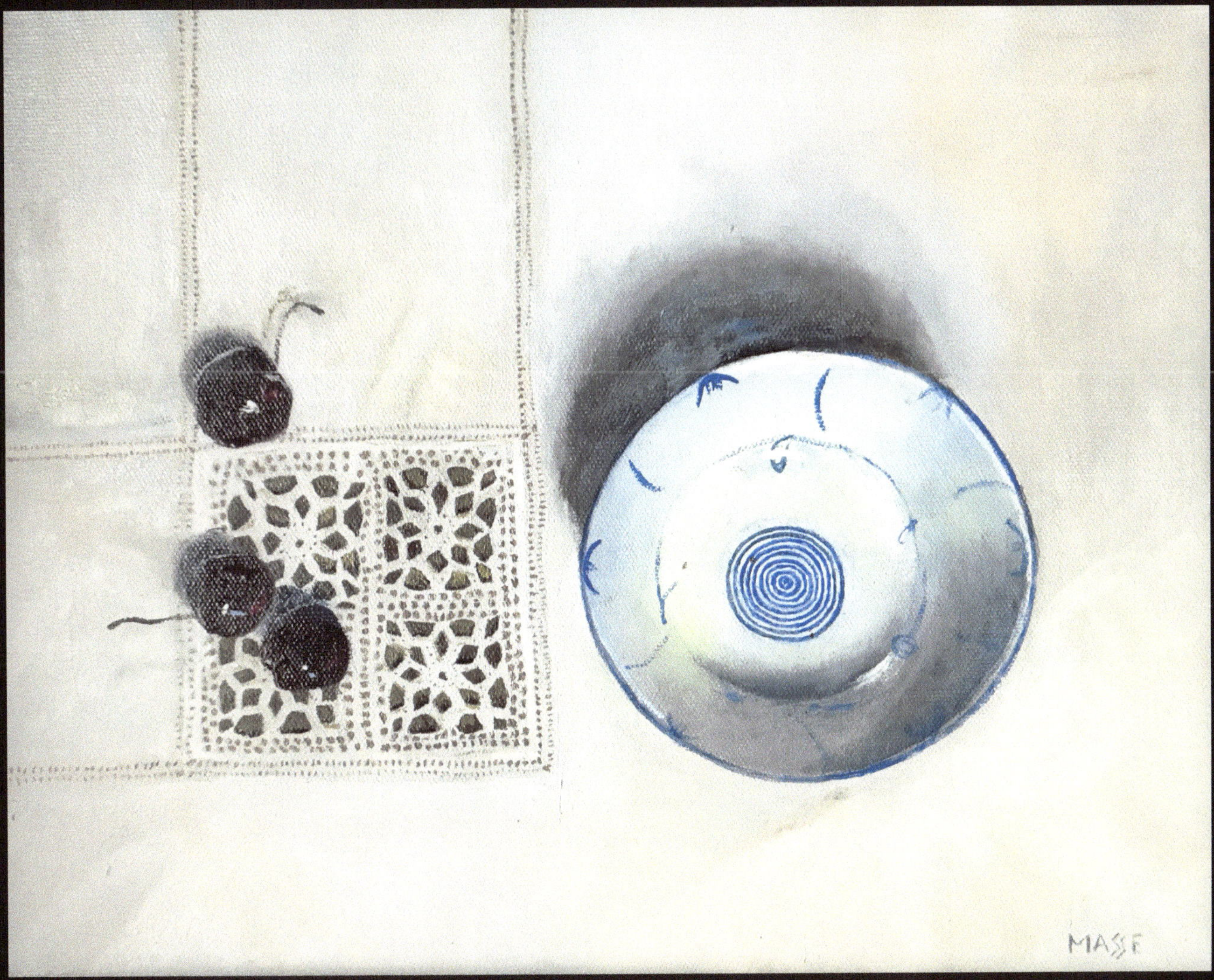

Susan Masse, Meme's Tablecloth, oil on canvas

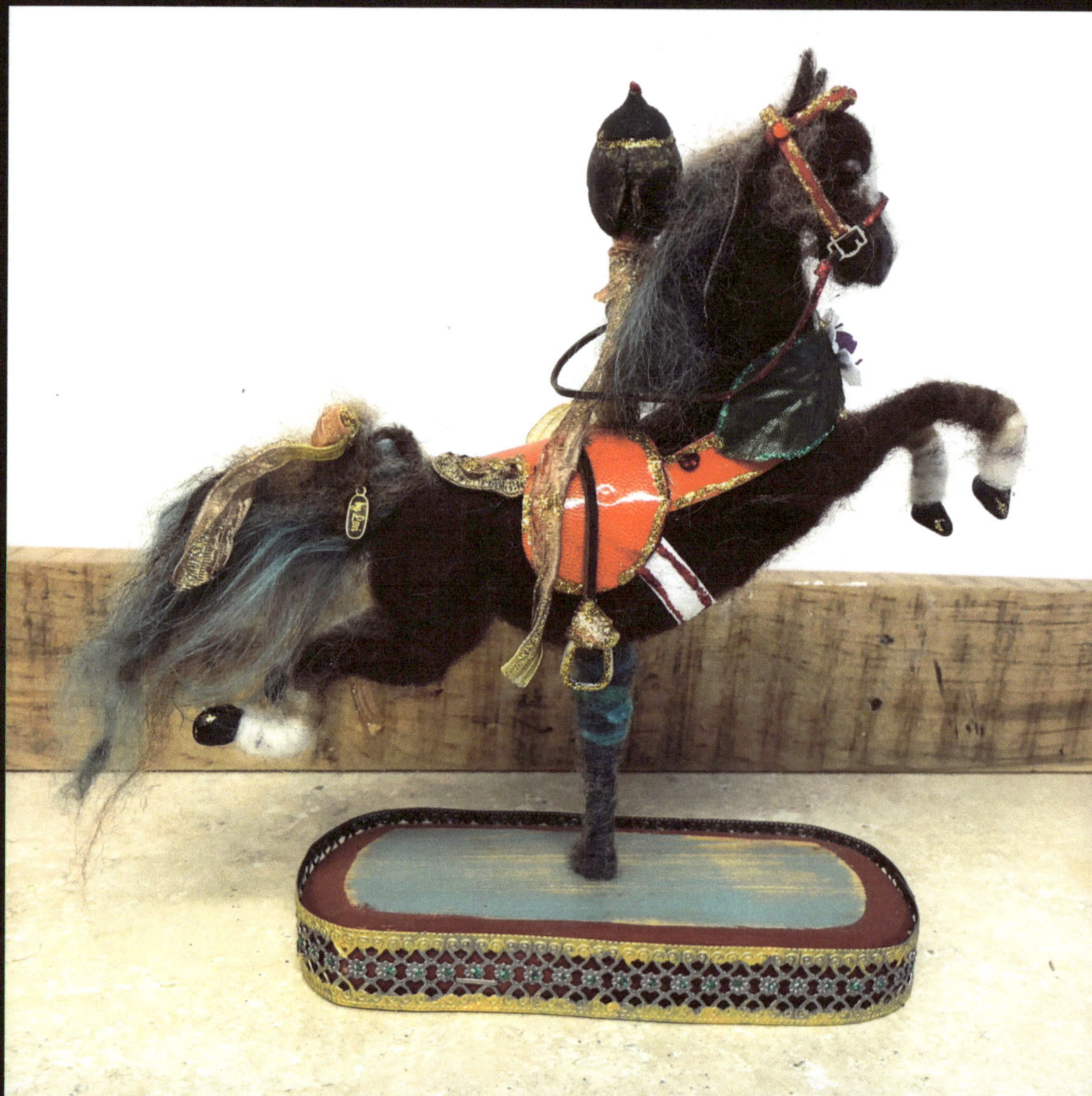

Lori Neumann, My Carousel, wool fiber and mixed media

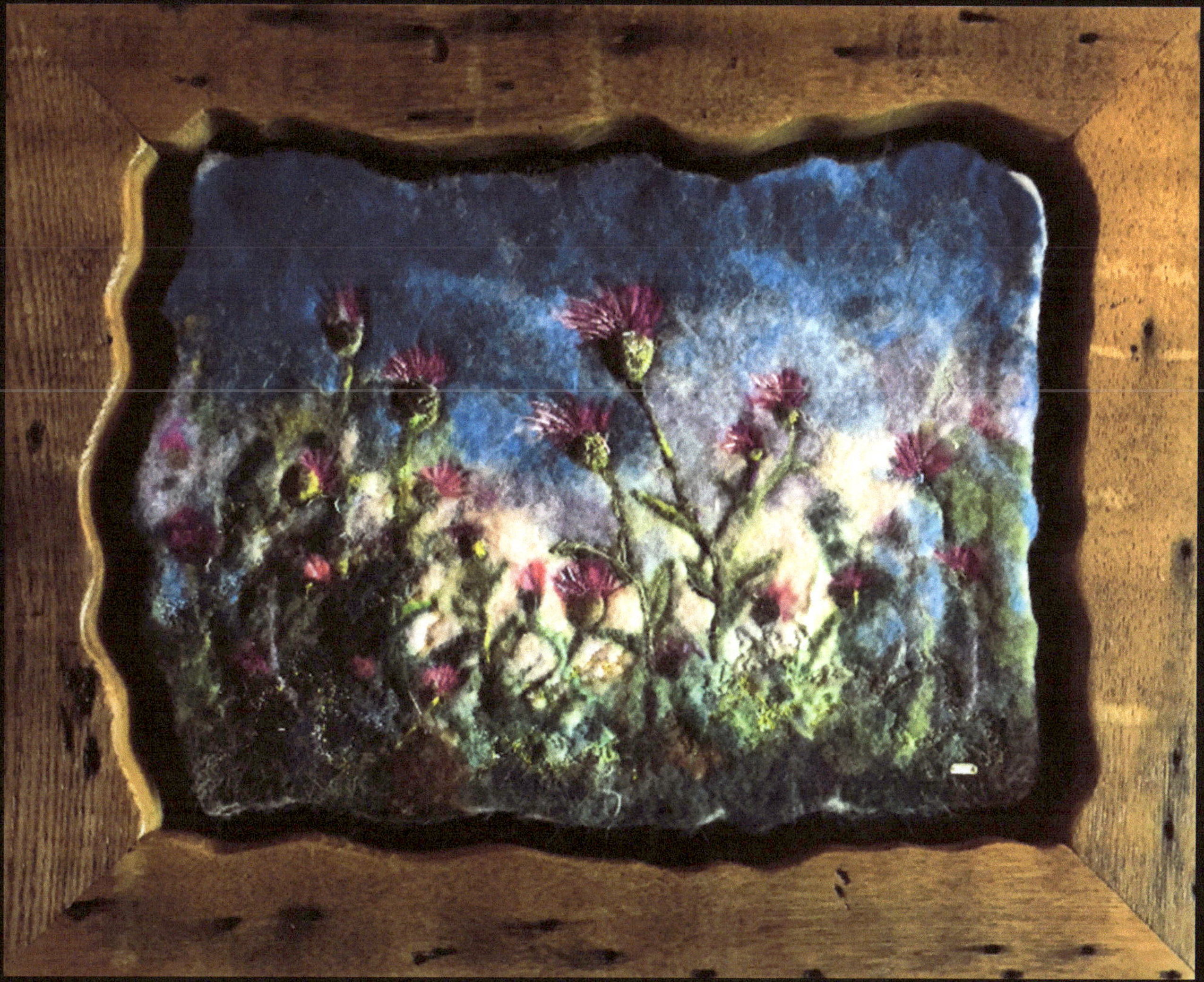

Lori Neumann, Thistles in the Wind, wet and dry felting

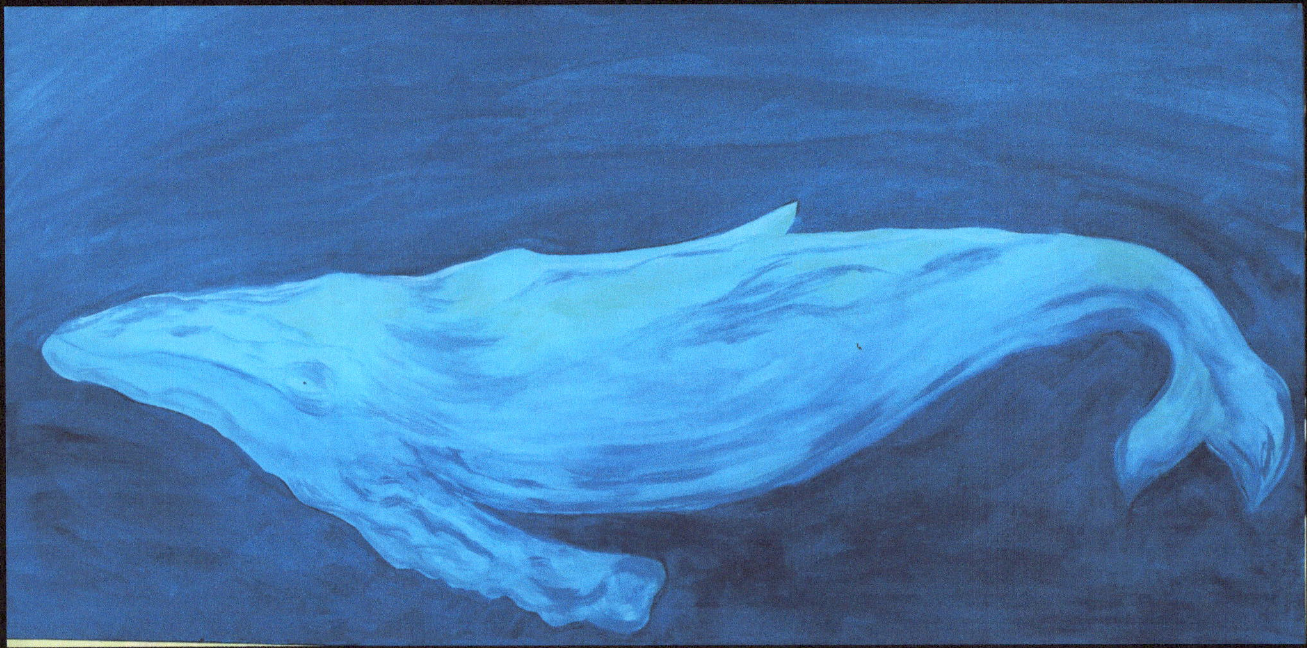

Marianne Nicholas, Humpback, acrylic on canvas

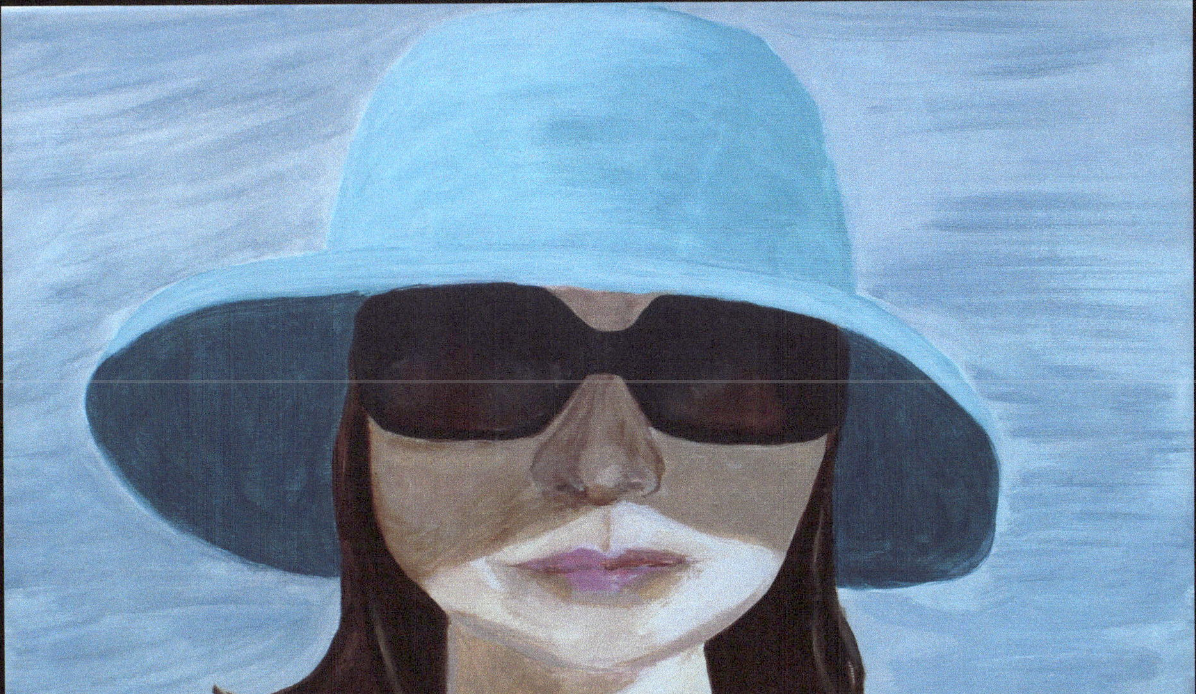

Marianne Nicholas, Self Portrait, acrylic on canvas

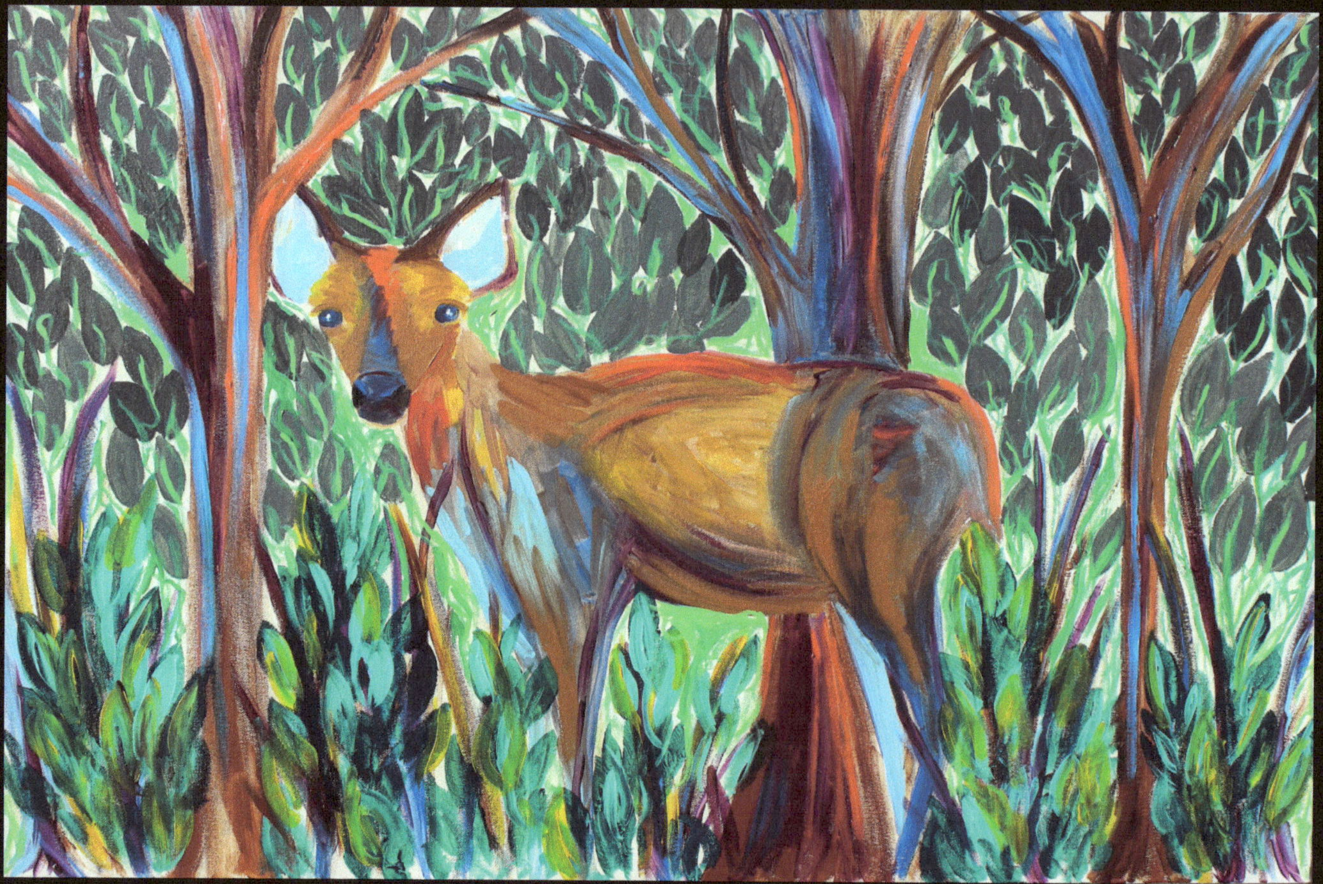

Marianne Nicholas, She Sees Us, acrylic on canvas

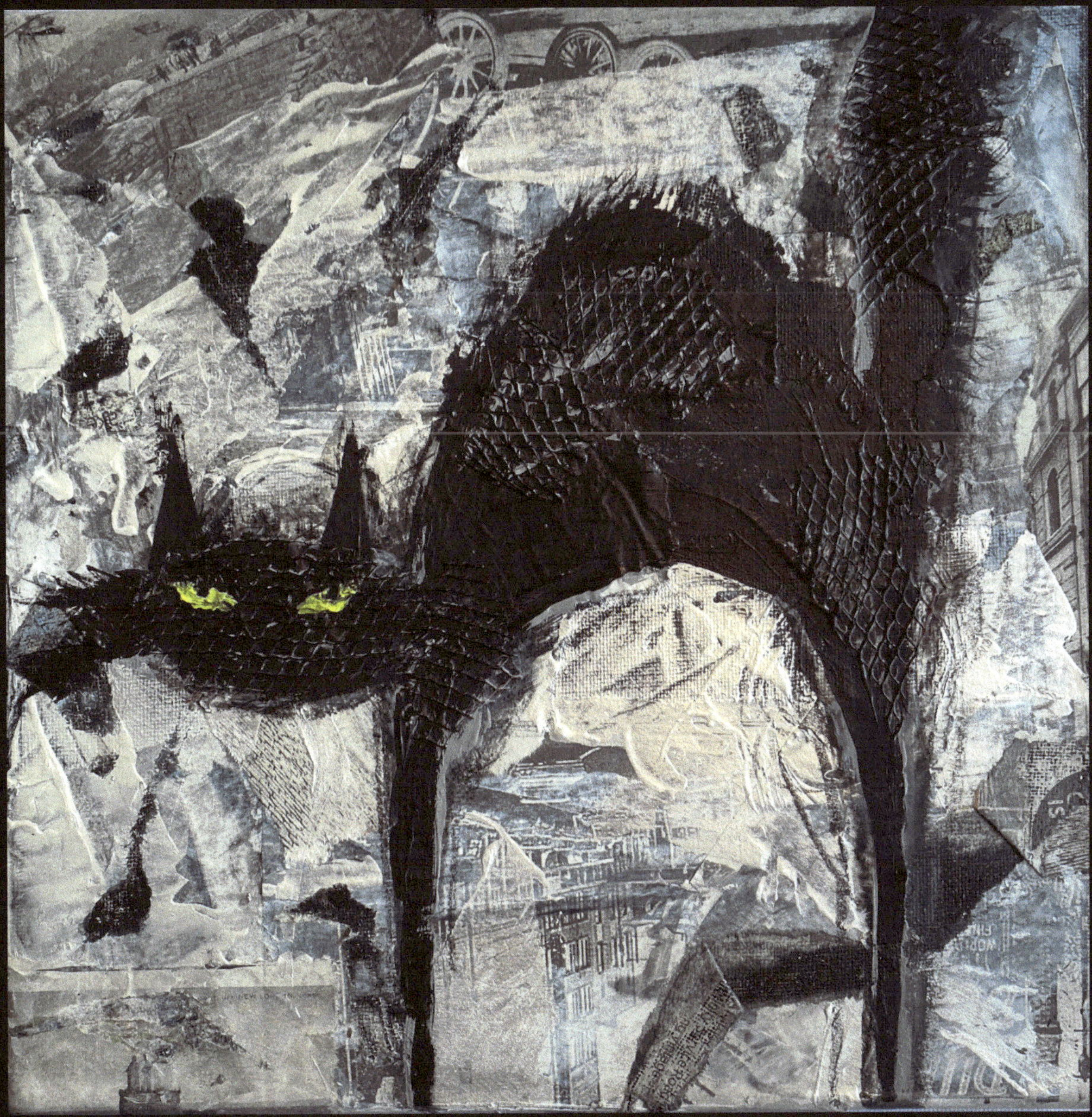

Marianne Nicholas, Stray, acrylic on canvas

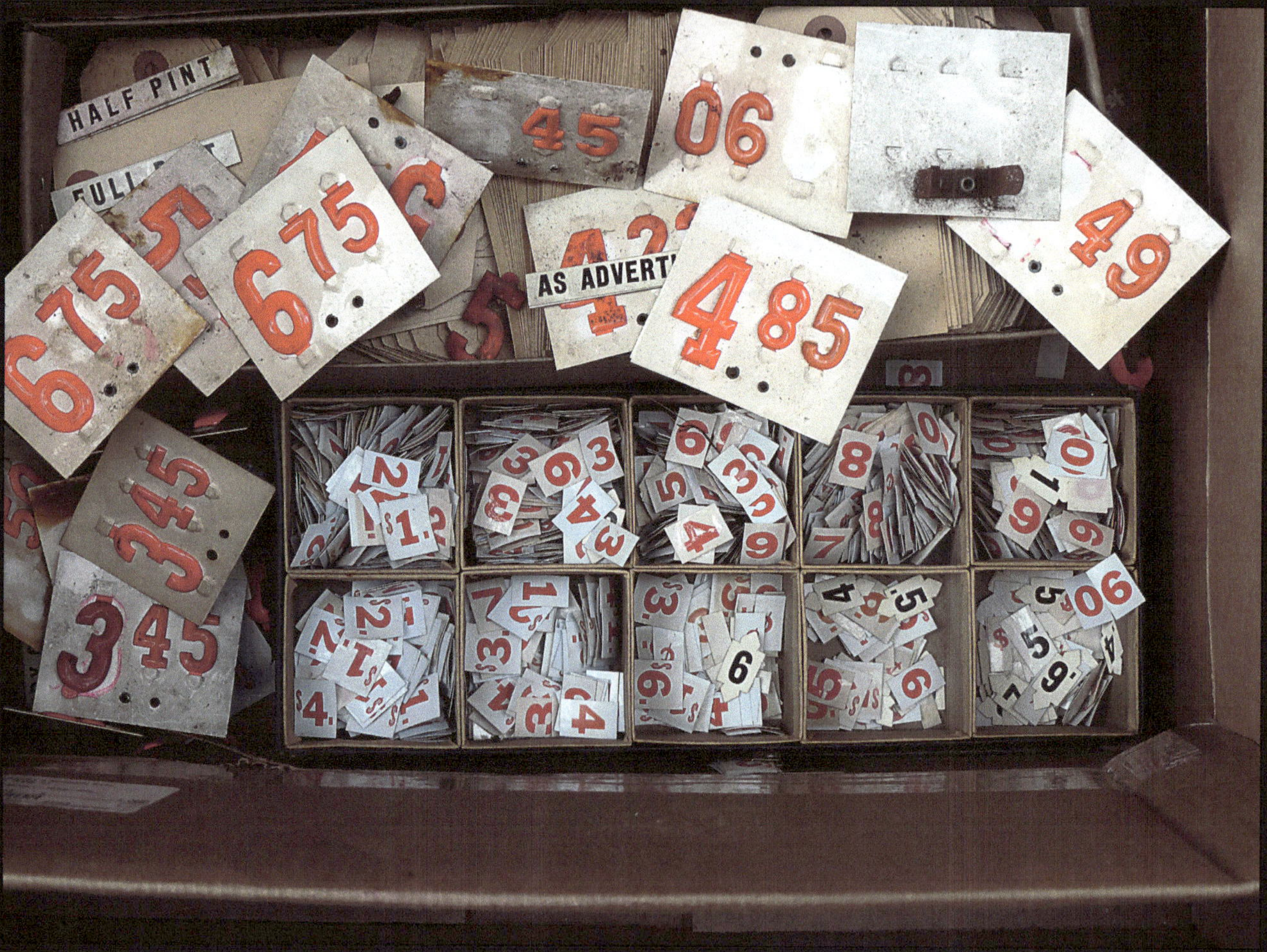

Susan Parish, Box of Numbers, photograph

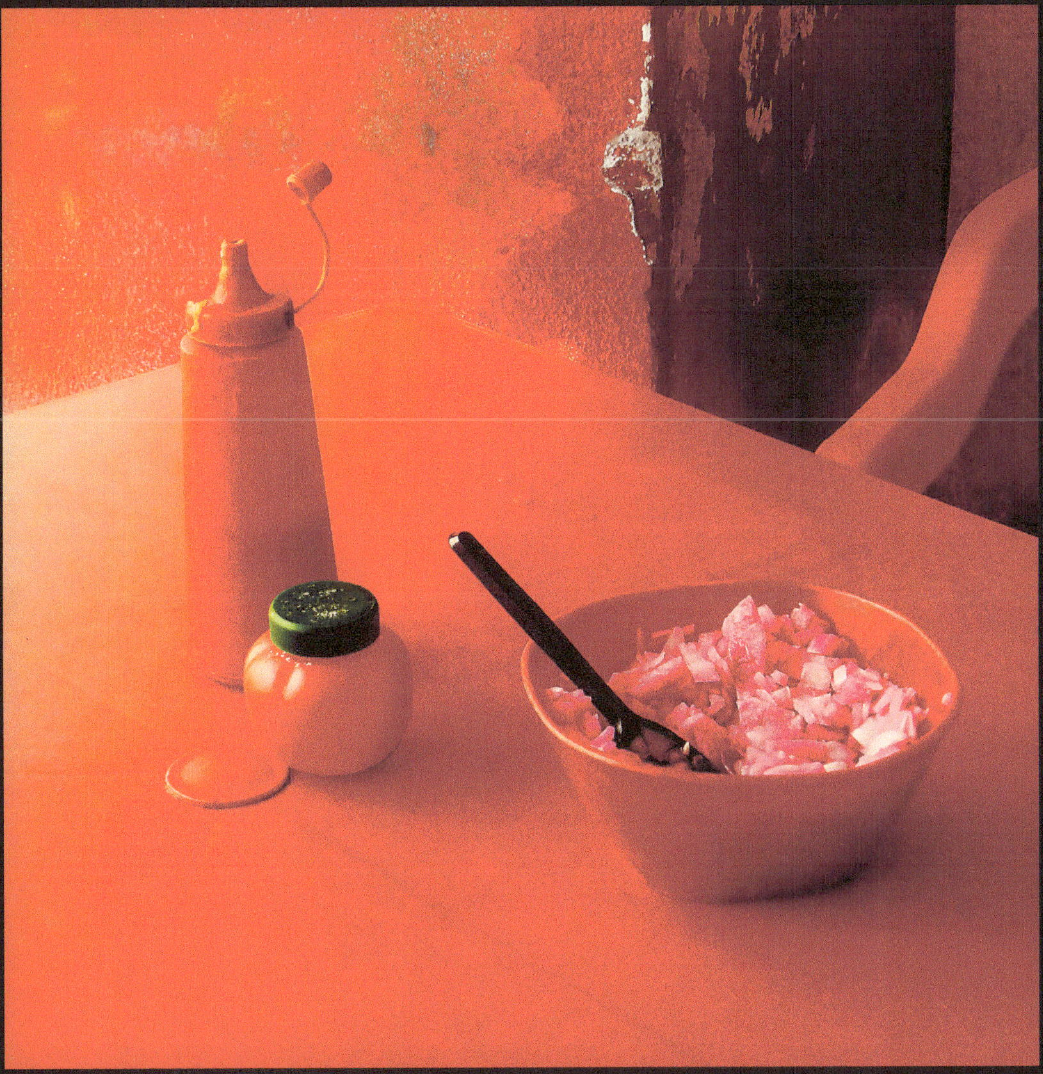

Susan Parish, Gorditas, photograph

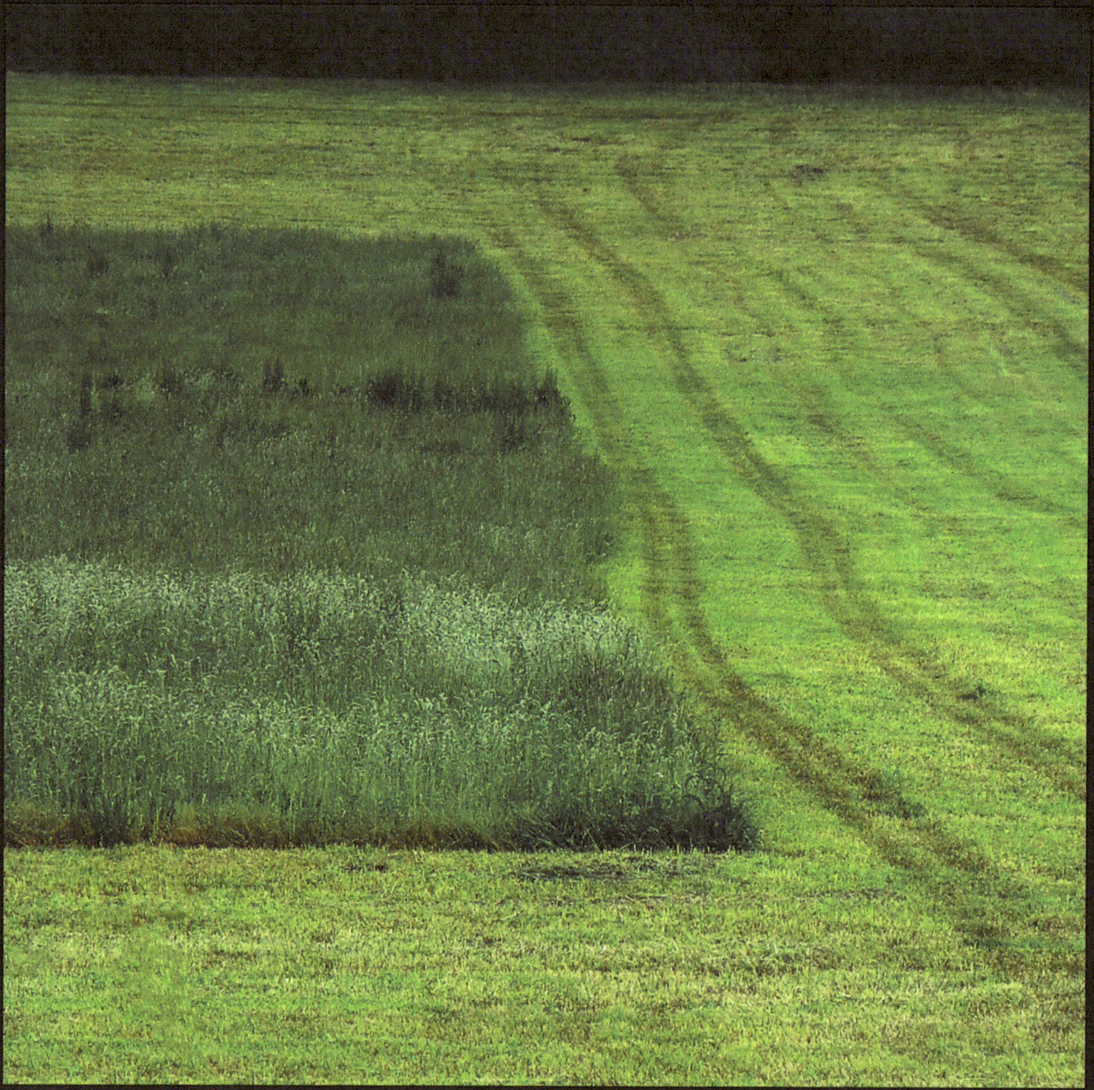

Susan Parish, Hayfield, photograph

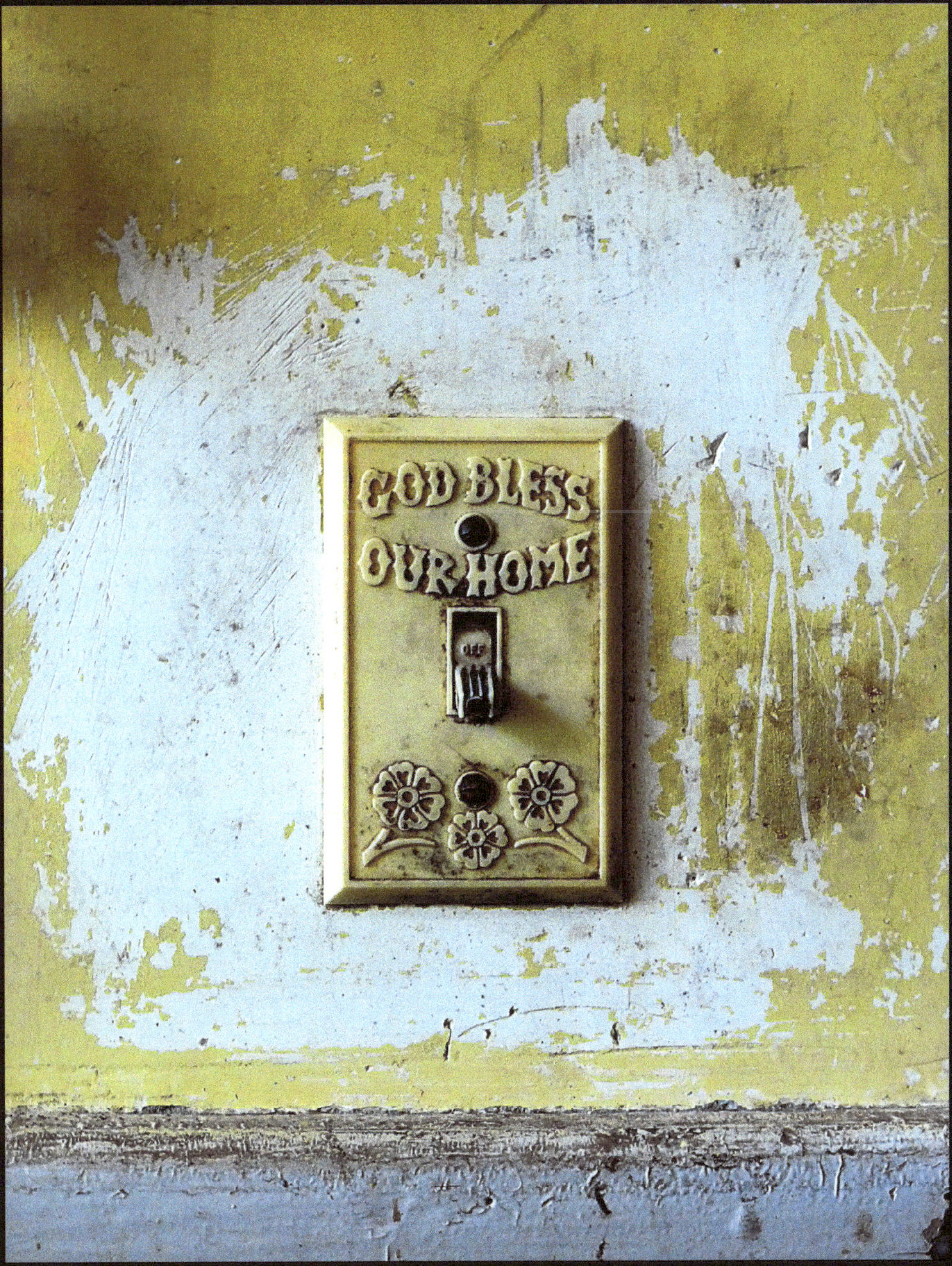

Susan Parish, Light Switch, photograph

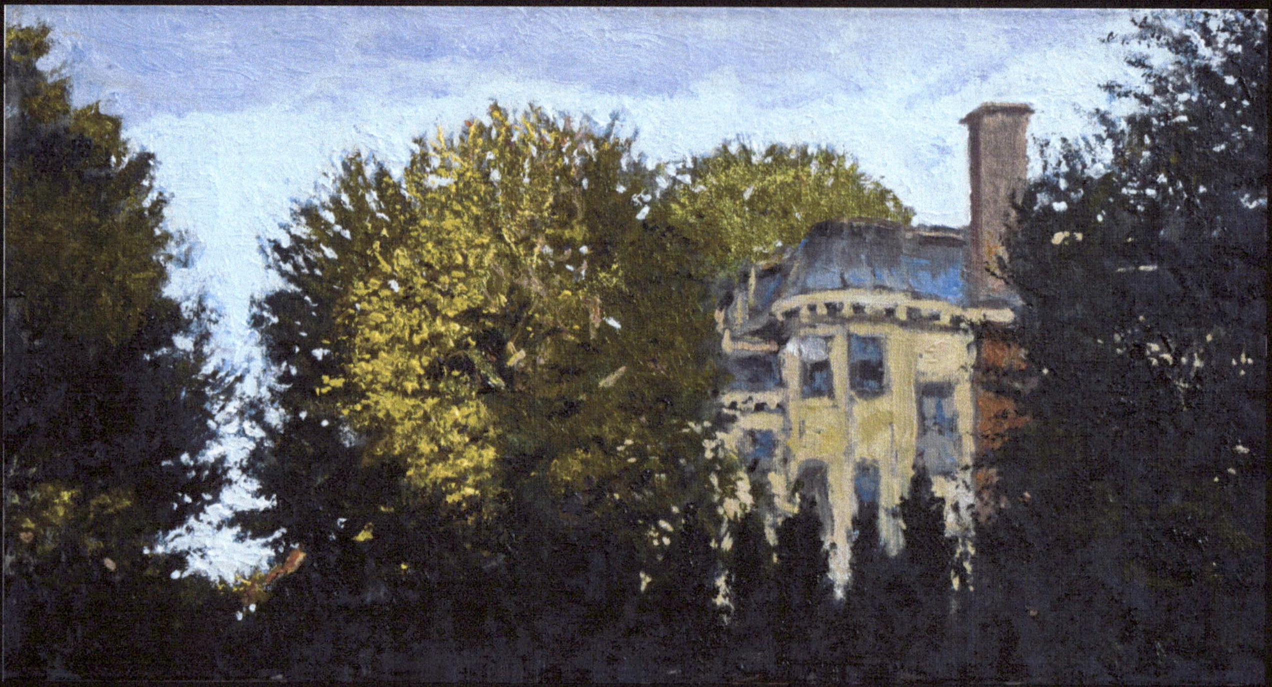

Mark Patnode, Evening Glow, oil on linen

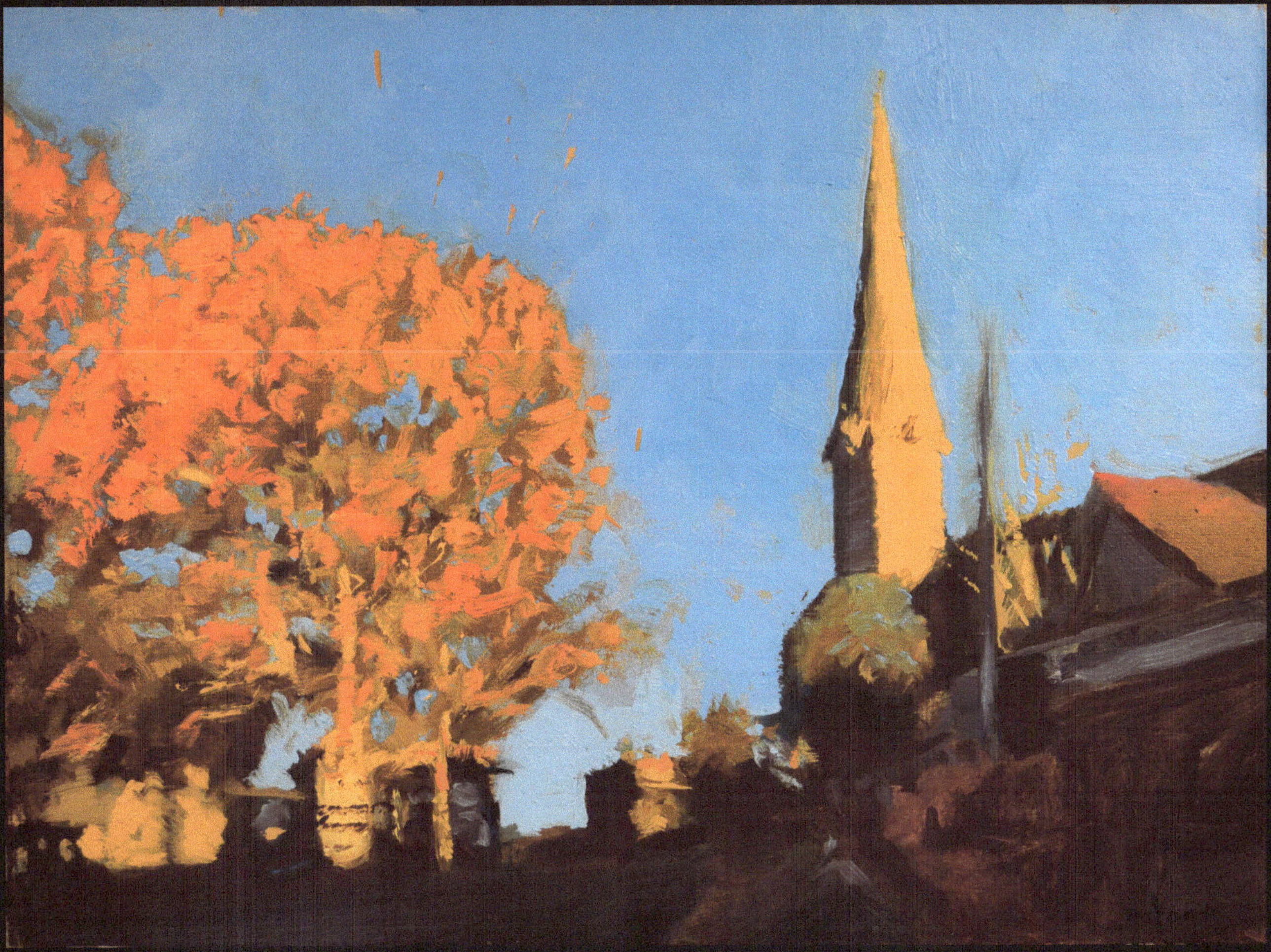

Mark Patnode, Autumn Sunrise, oil on linen

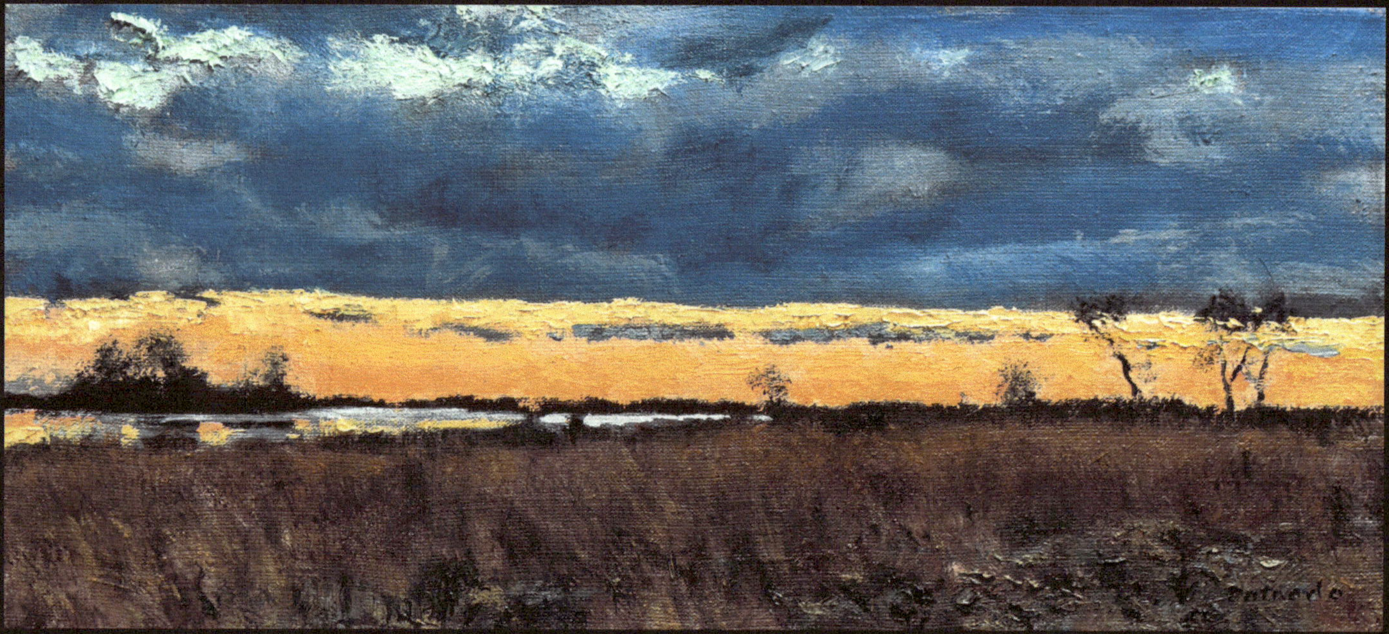

Mark Patnode, Goshen Cove, oil on linen

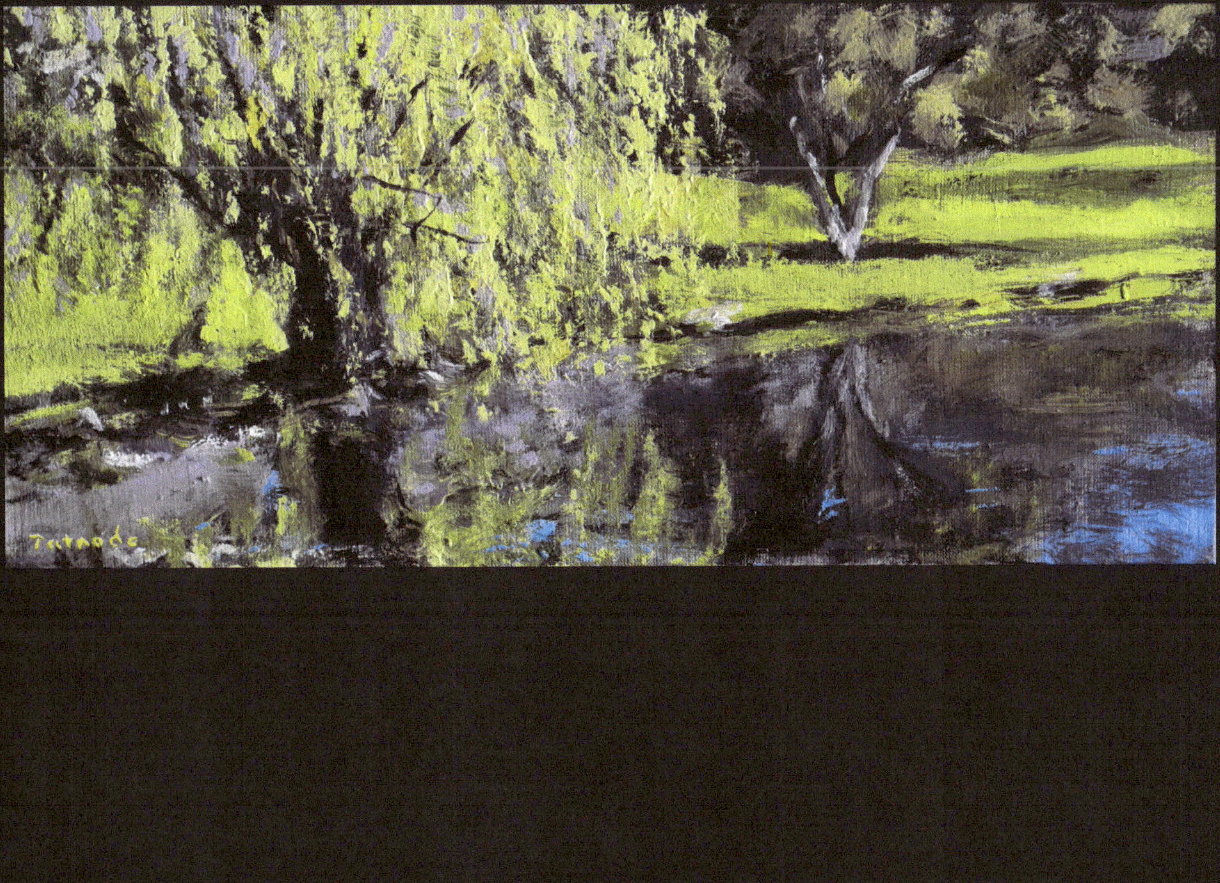

Mark Patnode, Shoreline - Tributary Mill, oil on linen

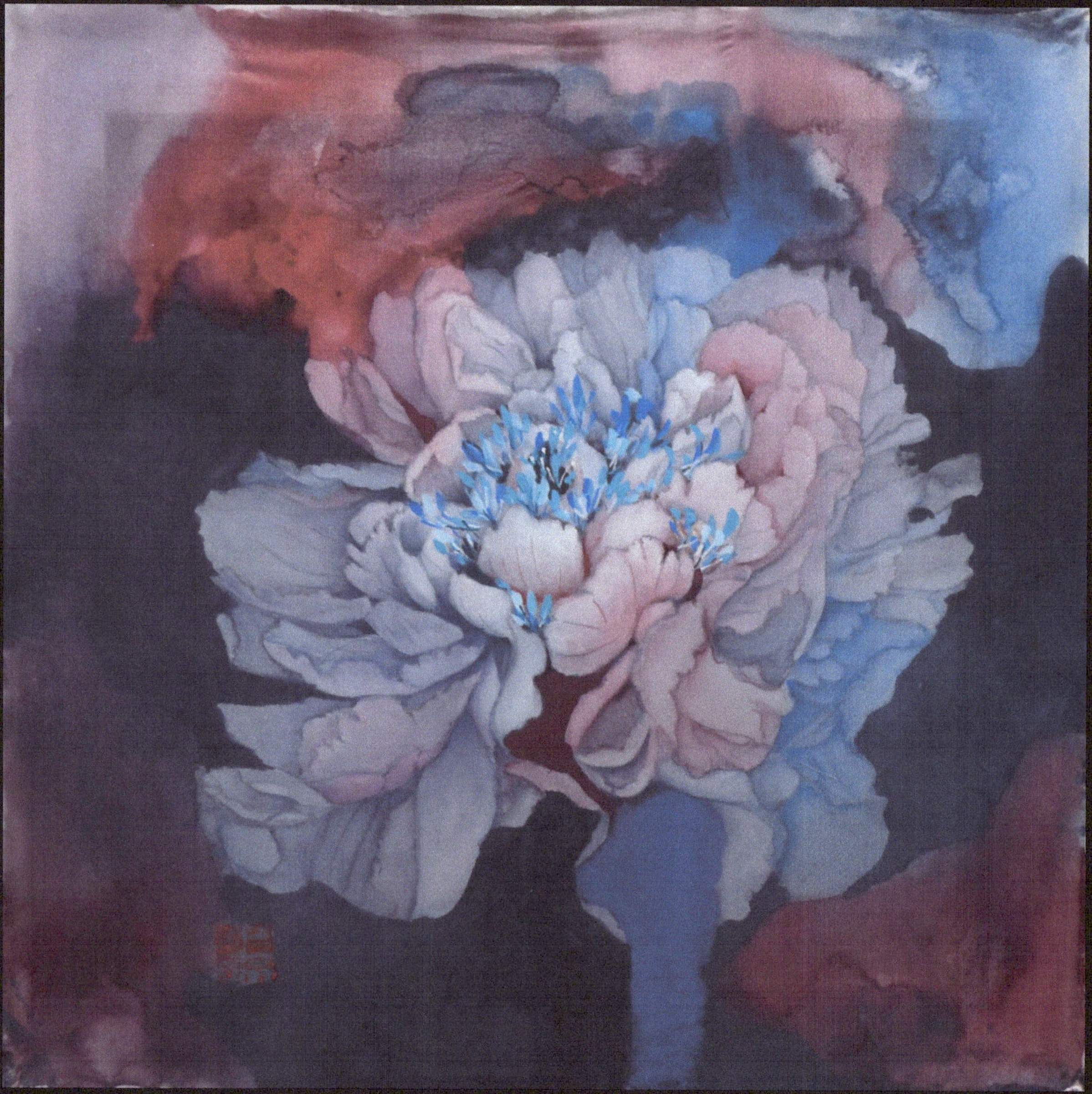

Yujuan Patnode, Flower in Rainbow, watercolor on silk

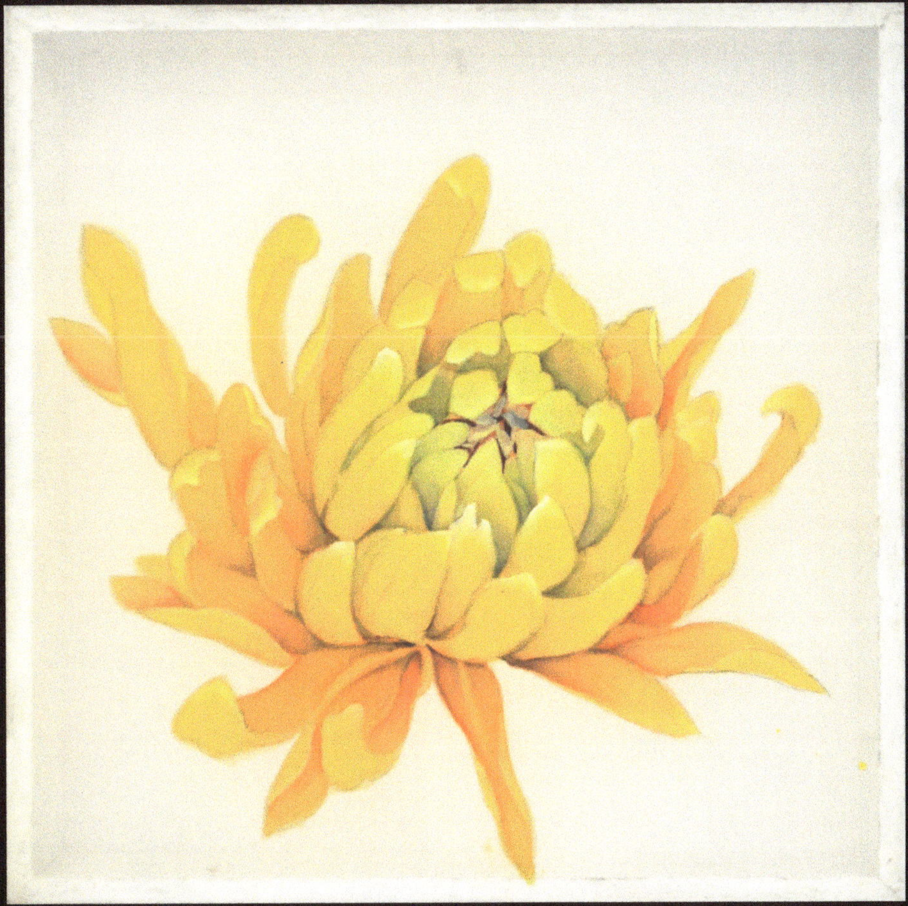

Yujuan Patnode, Memory of Autumn, watercolor on silk

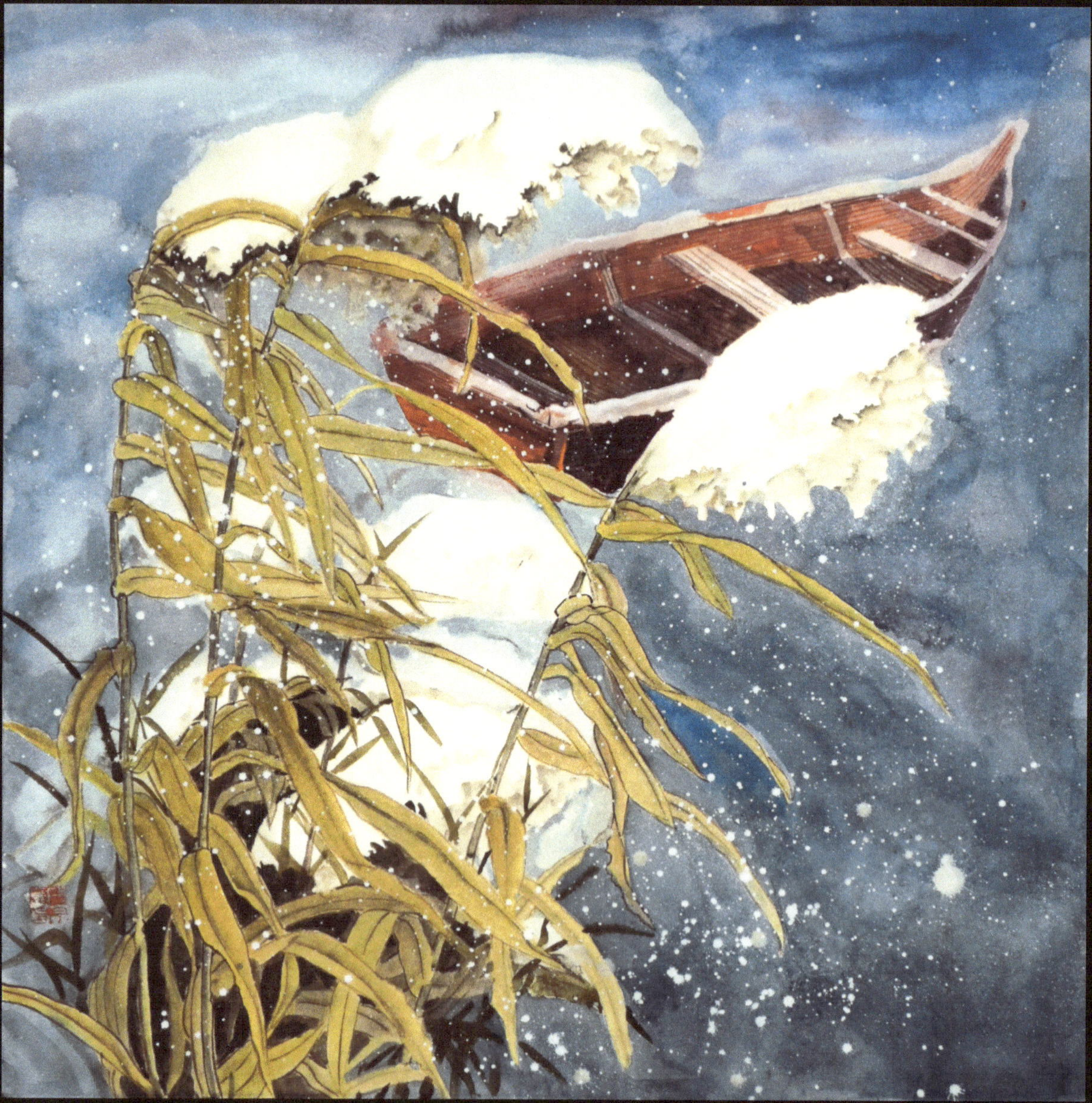

Yujuan Patnode, Winter, watercolor on paper

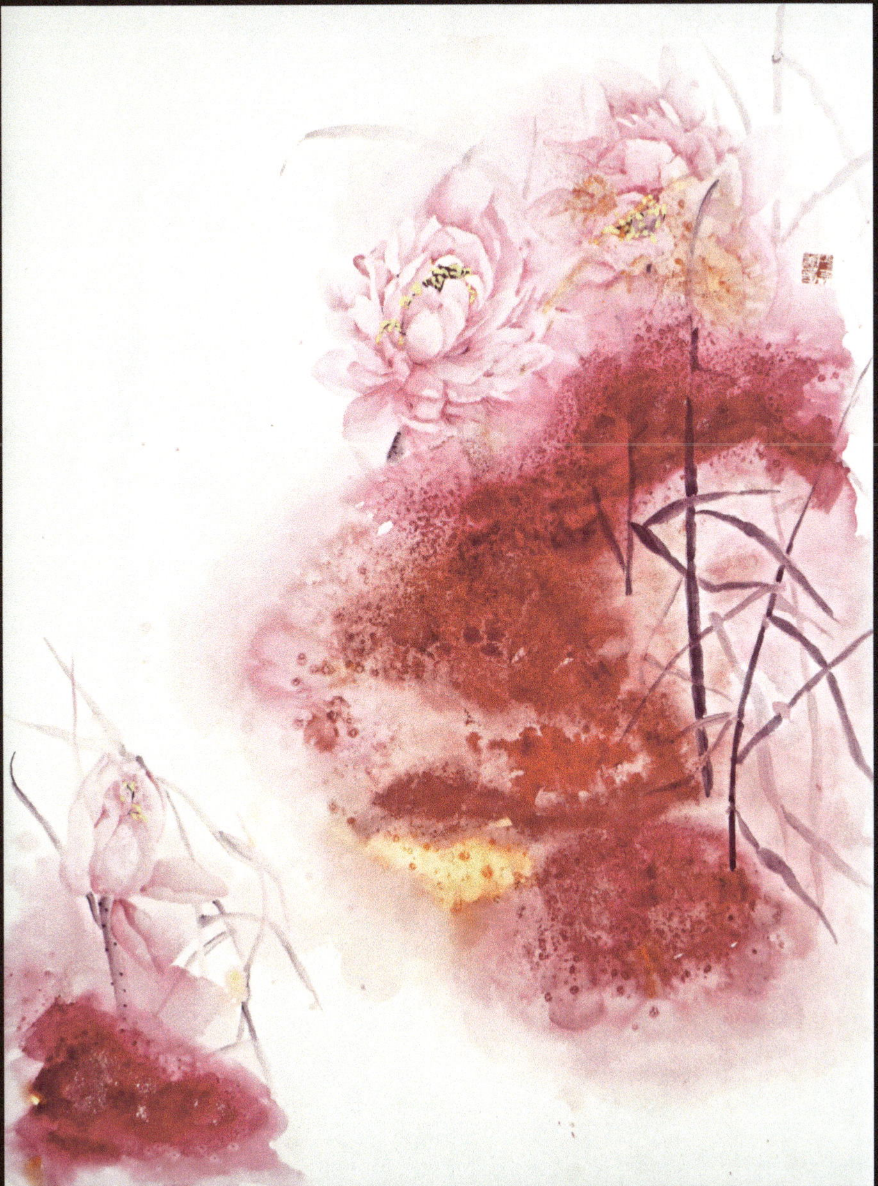

Yujuan Patnode, Sunset - Lotus Flower, watercolor on paper

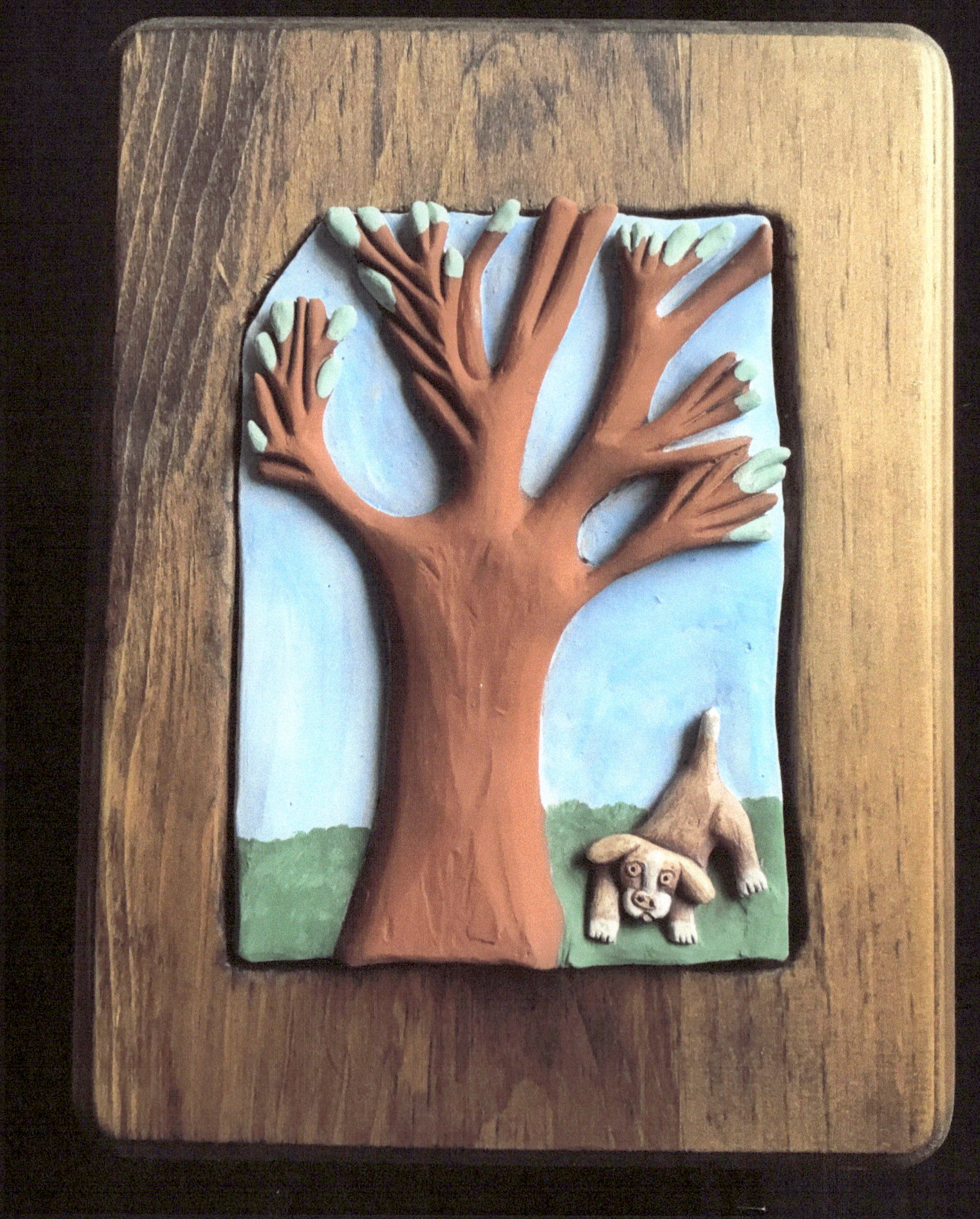

Lori Rembetski, Unleashed, terra cotta with iron oxide wash

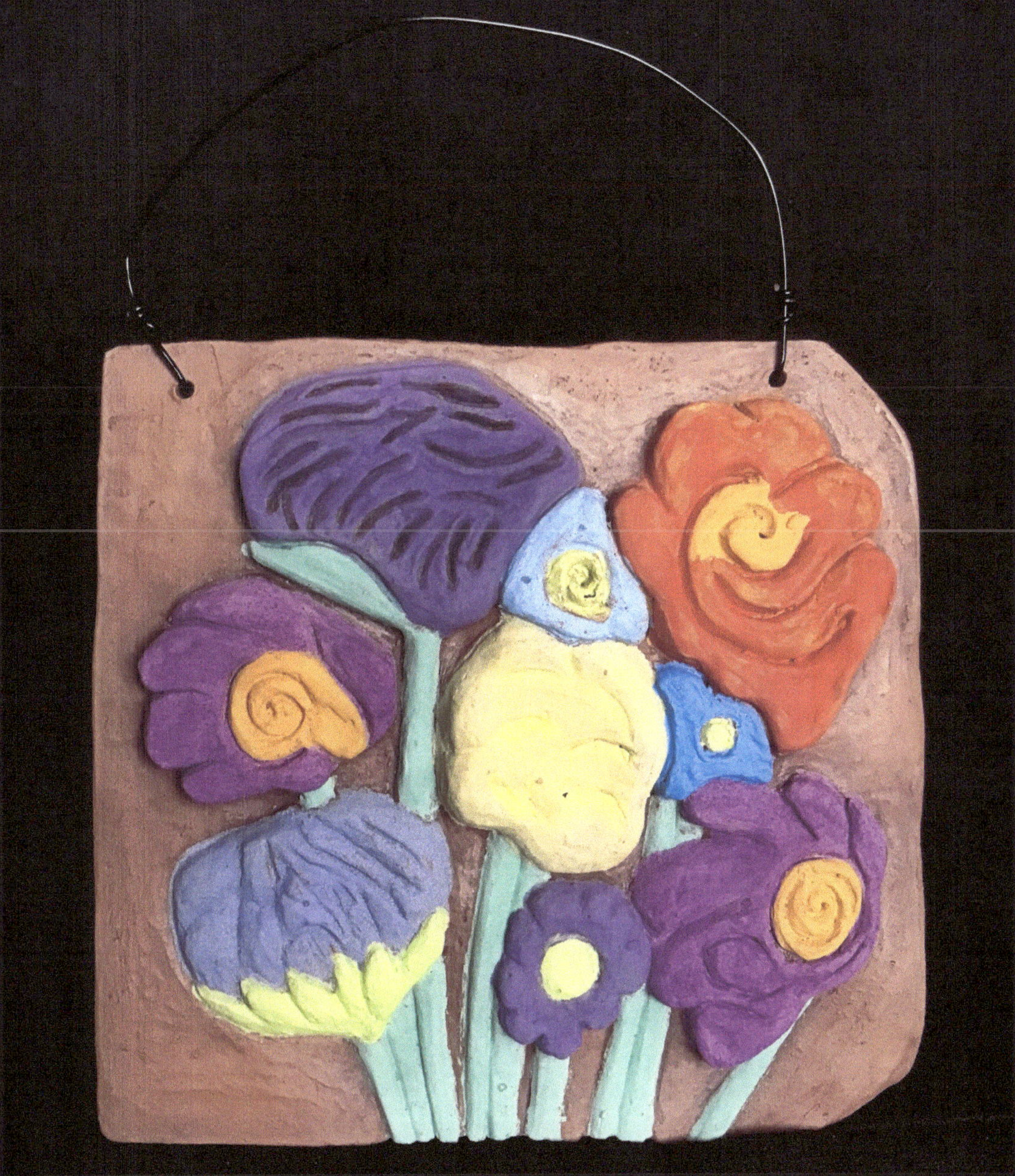

Lori Rembetski, Flower Bouquet, terra cotta
with iron oxide wash and under glaze

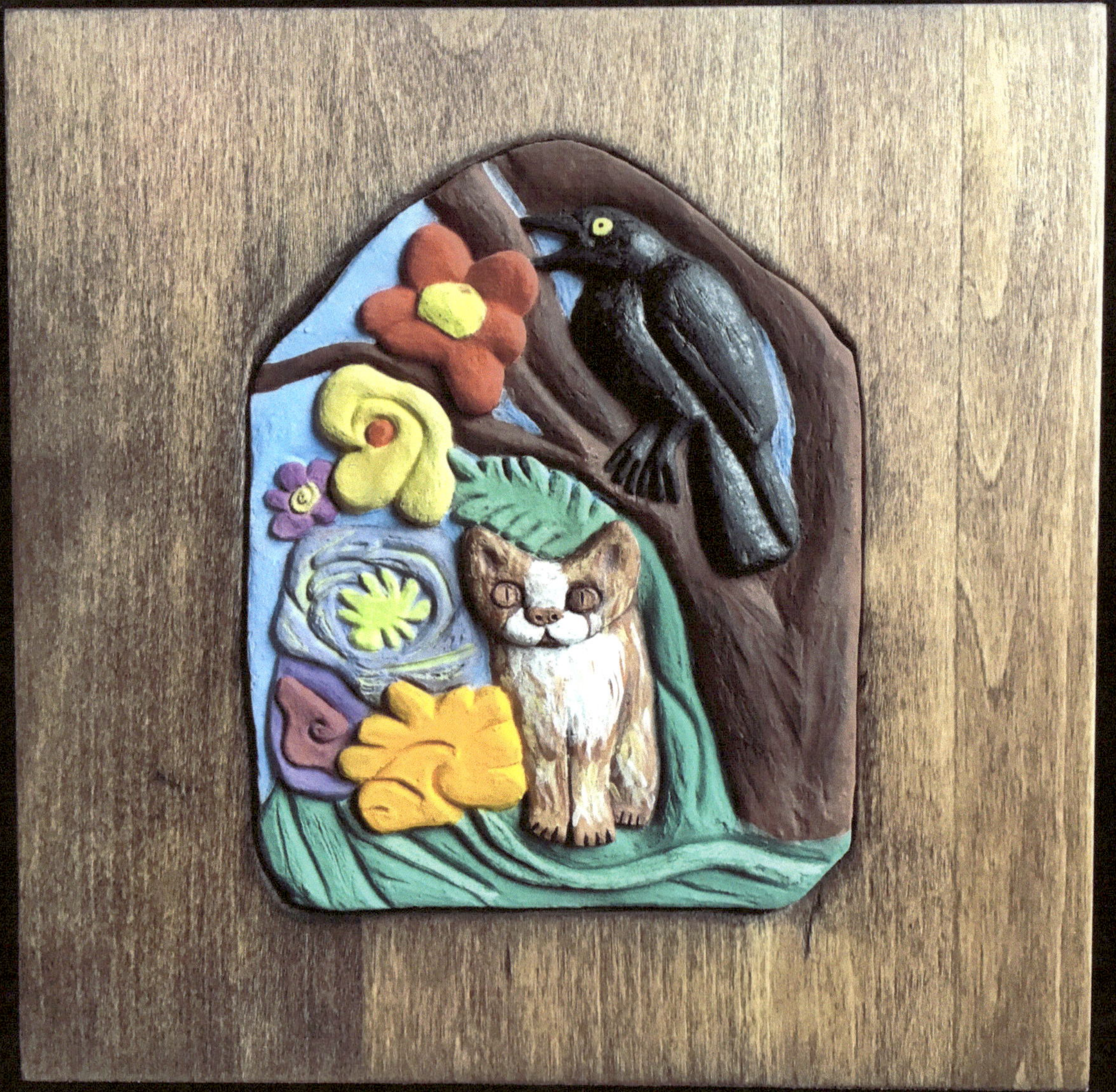

Lori Rembetski, Kitty's Big Day Out,
terra cotta with iron oxide wash and under glaze

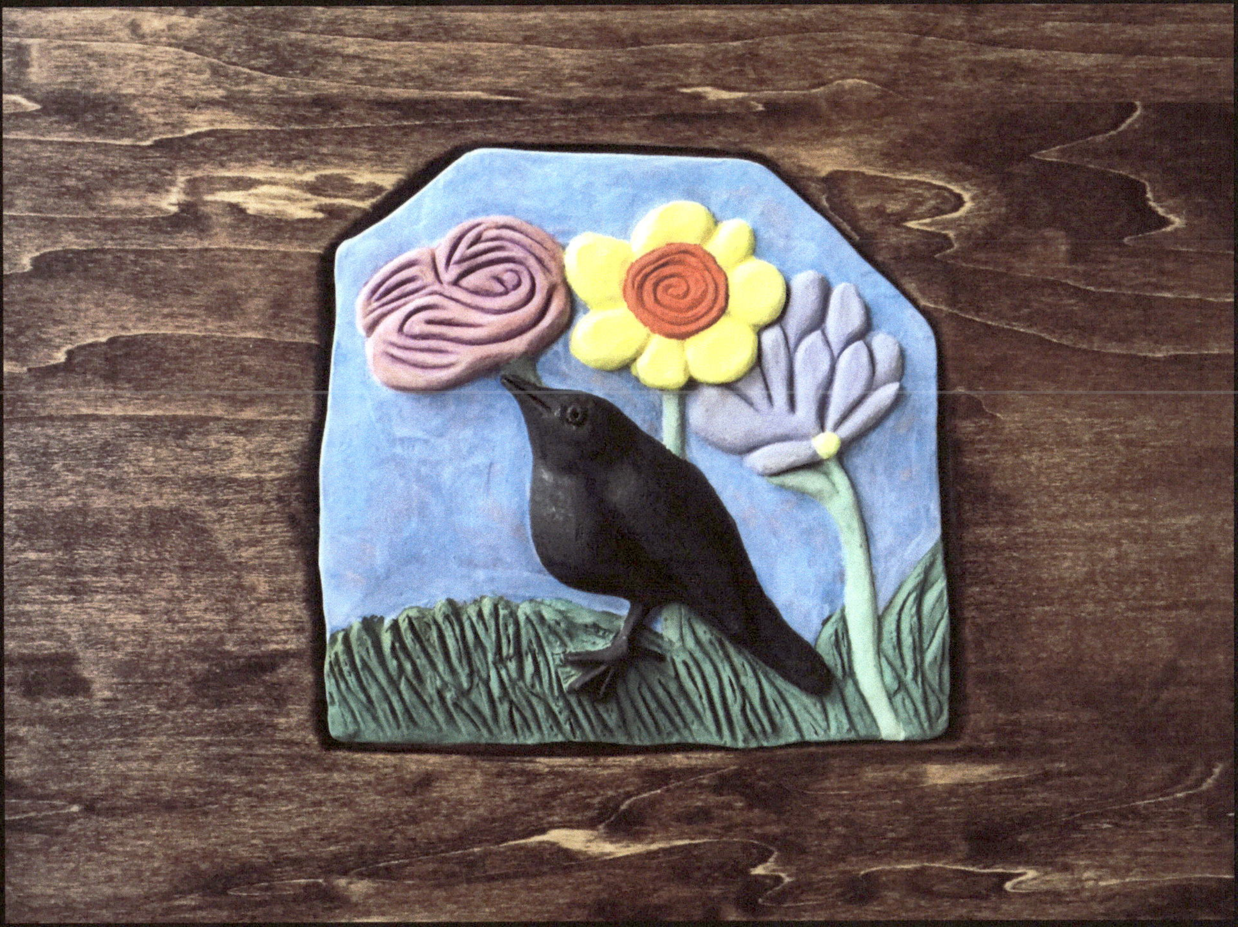

Lori Rembetski, In Full Bloom, terra cotta with under glaze & wood

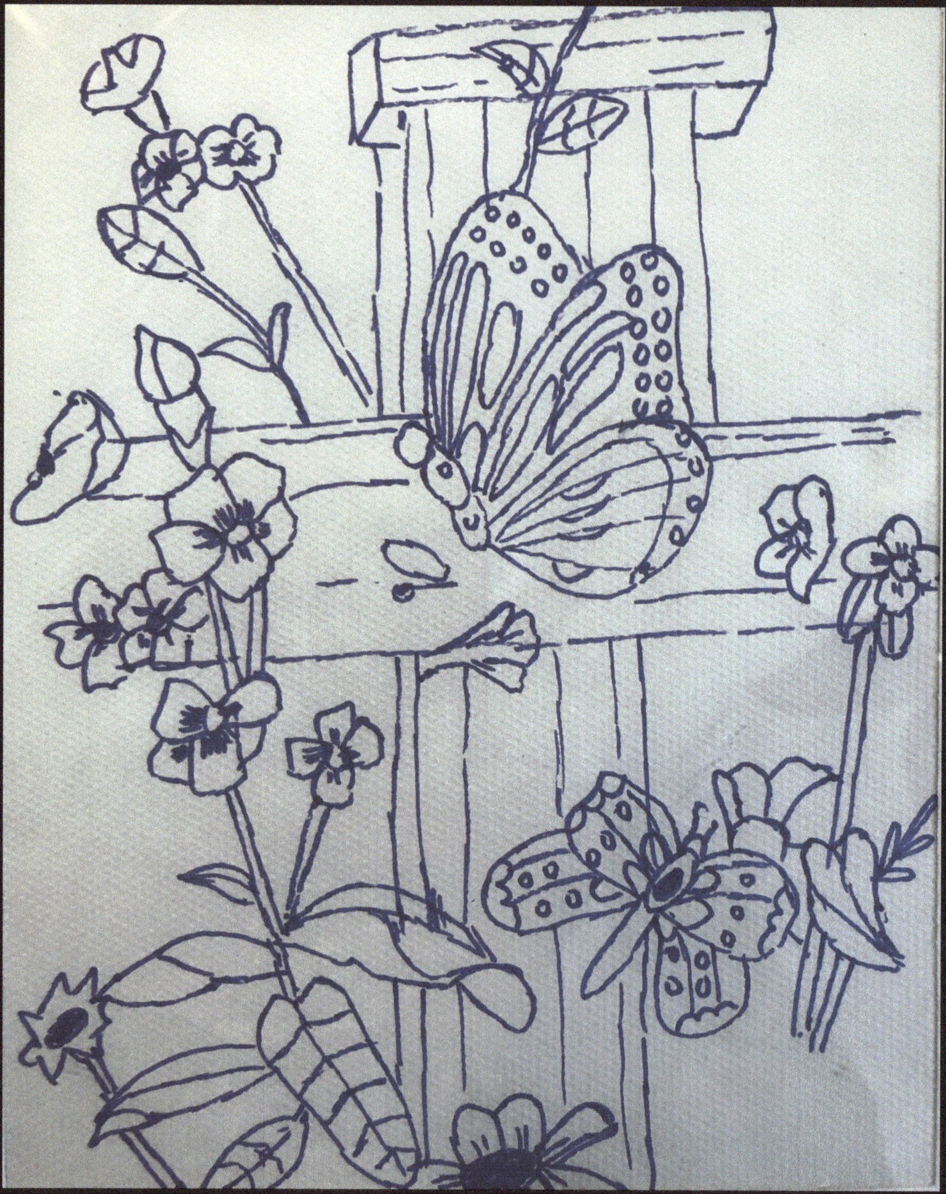

Lisa Shasha, Springtime, marker on paper

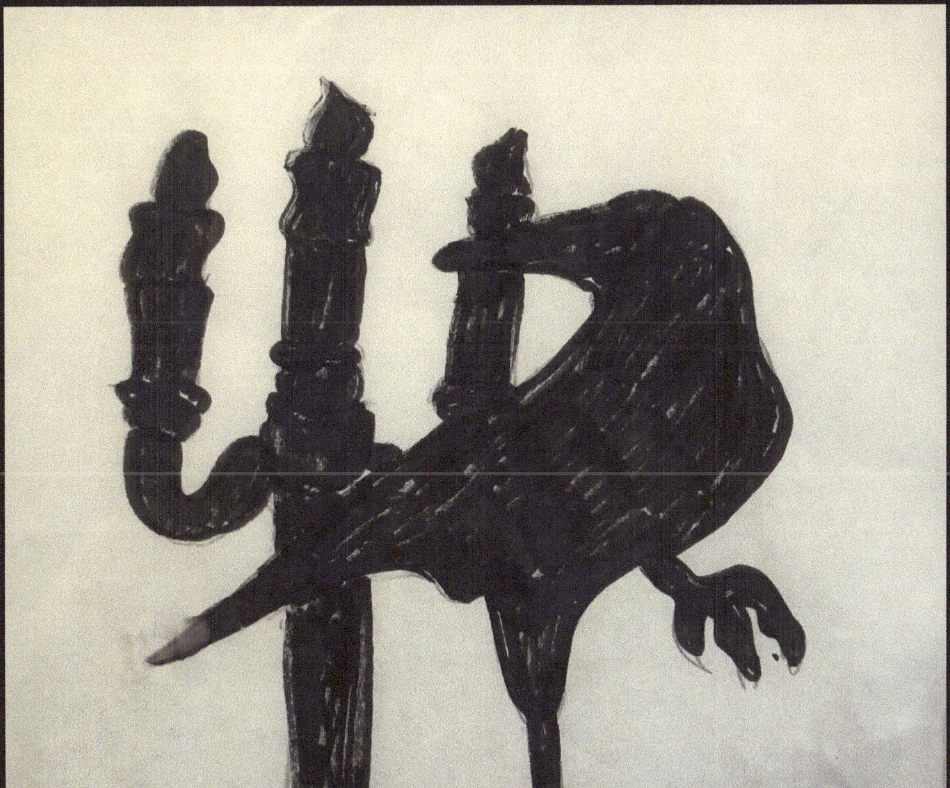

Lisa Shasha, Candelabra with Raven, marker on paper

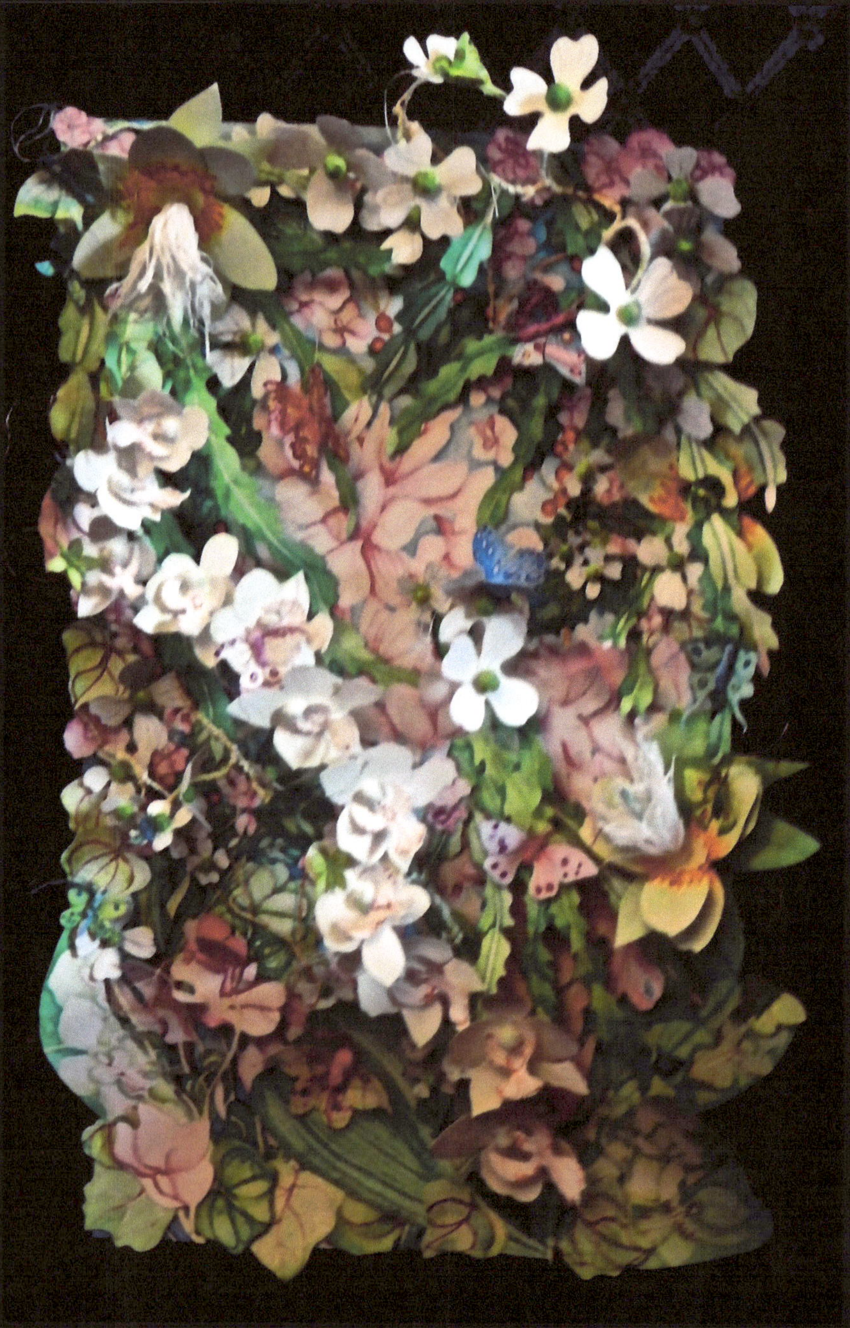

Gretchen van der Lyke, Northeast Spring, watercolor, cotton, wire

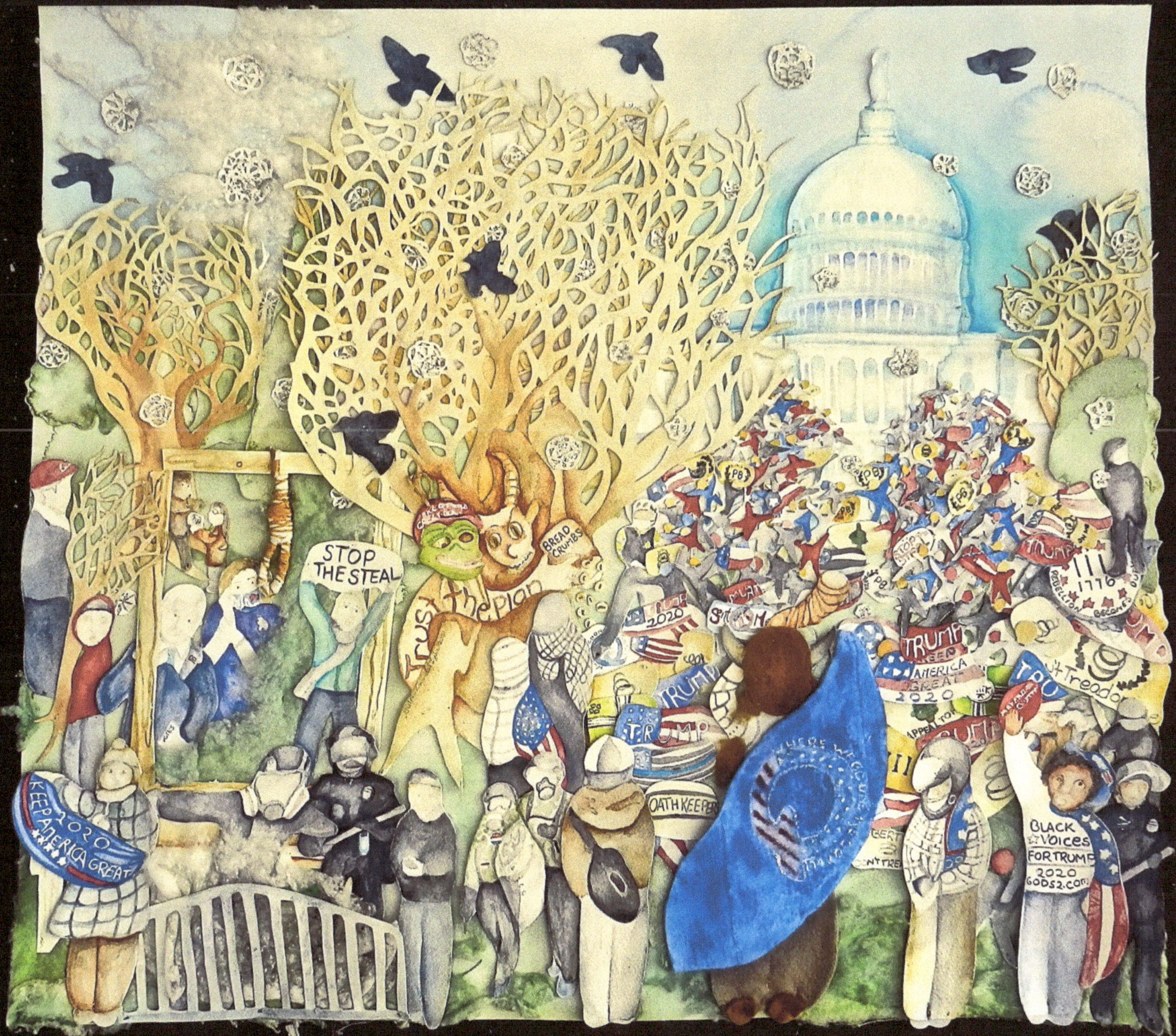

Gretchen van der Lyke, Maga Unmasked, watercolor, yarn, cotton

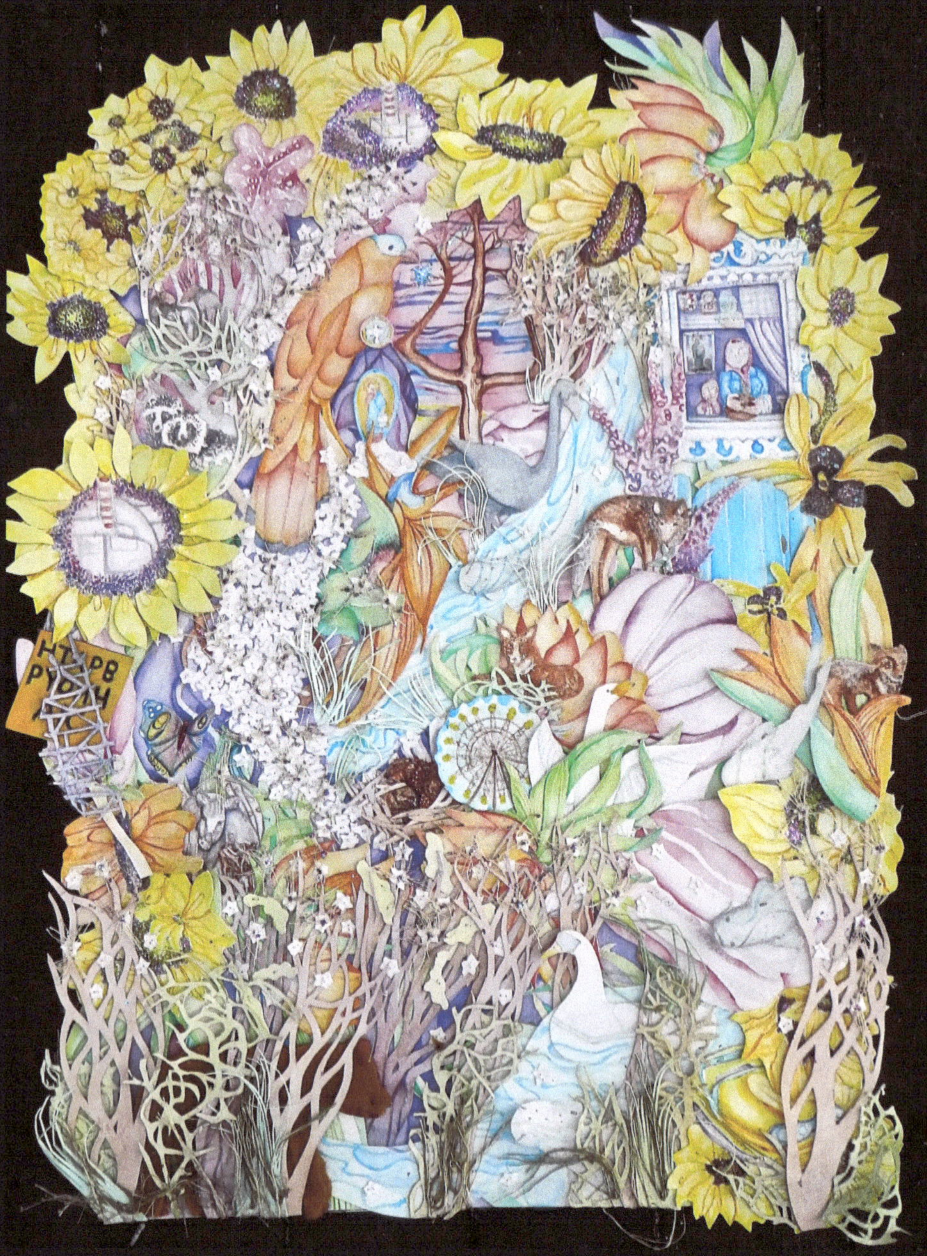

Gretchen van der Lyke, Three Days Extended, watercolor, thread, glitter

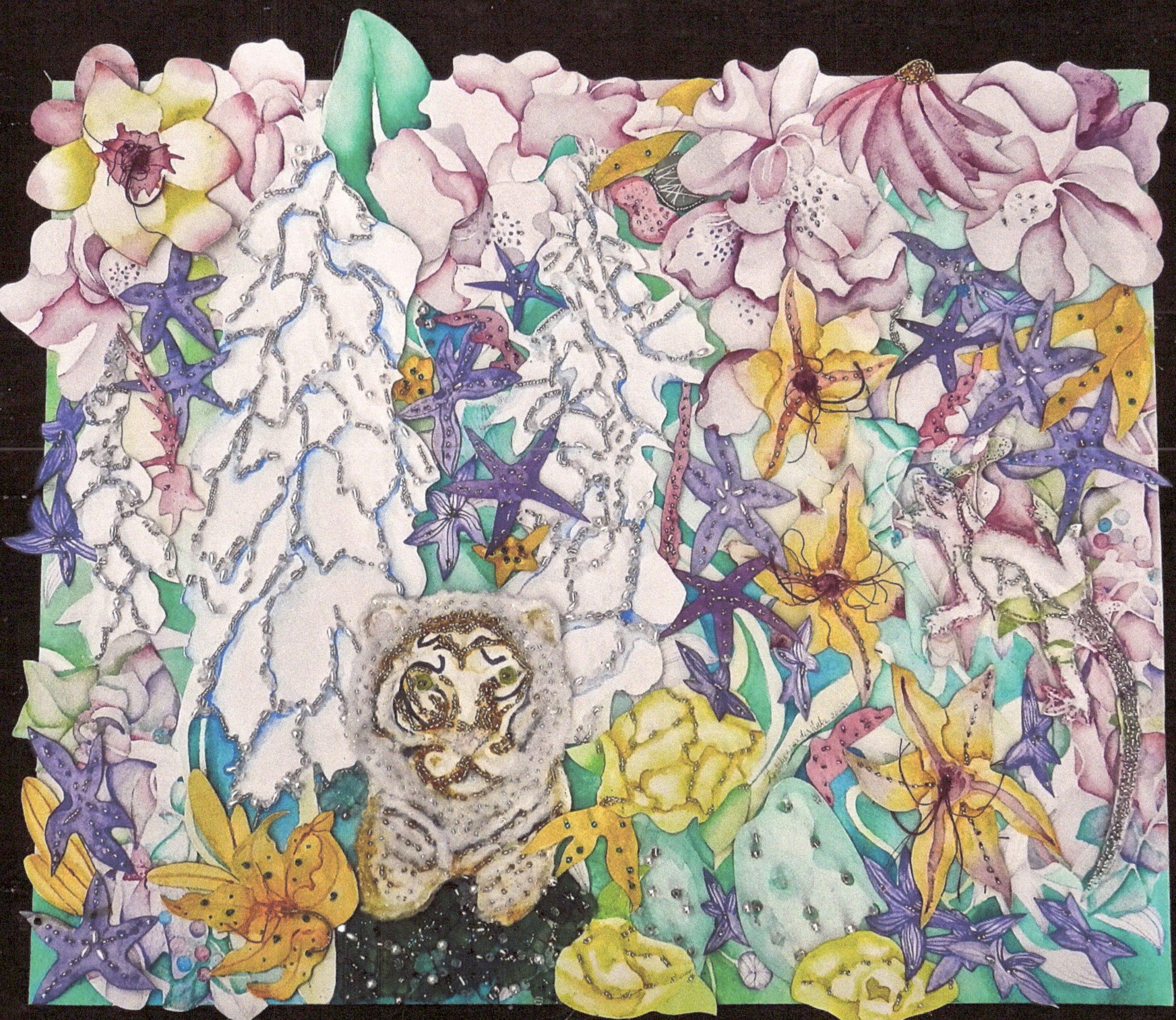

Gretchen van der Lyke, Inner and Outer States, watercolor, beads, seaglass

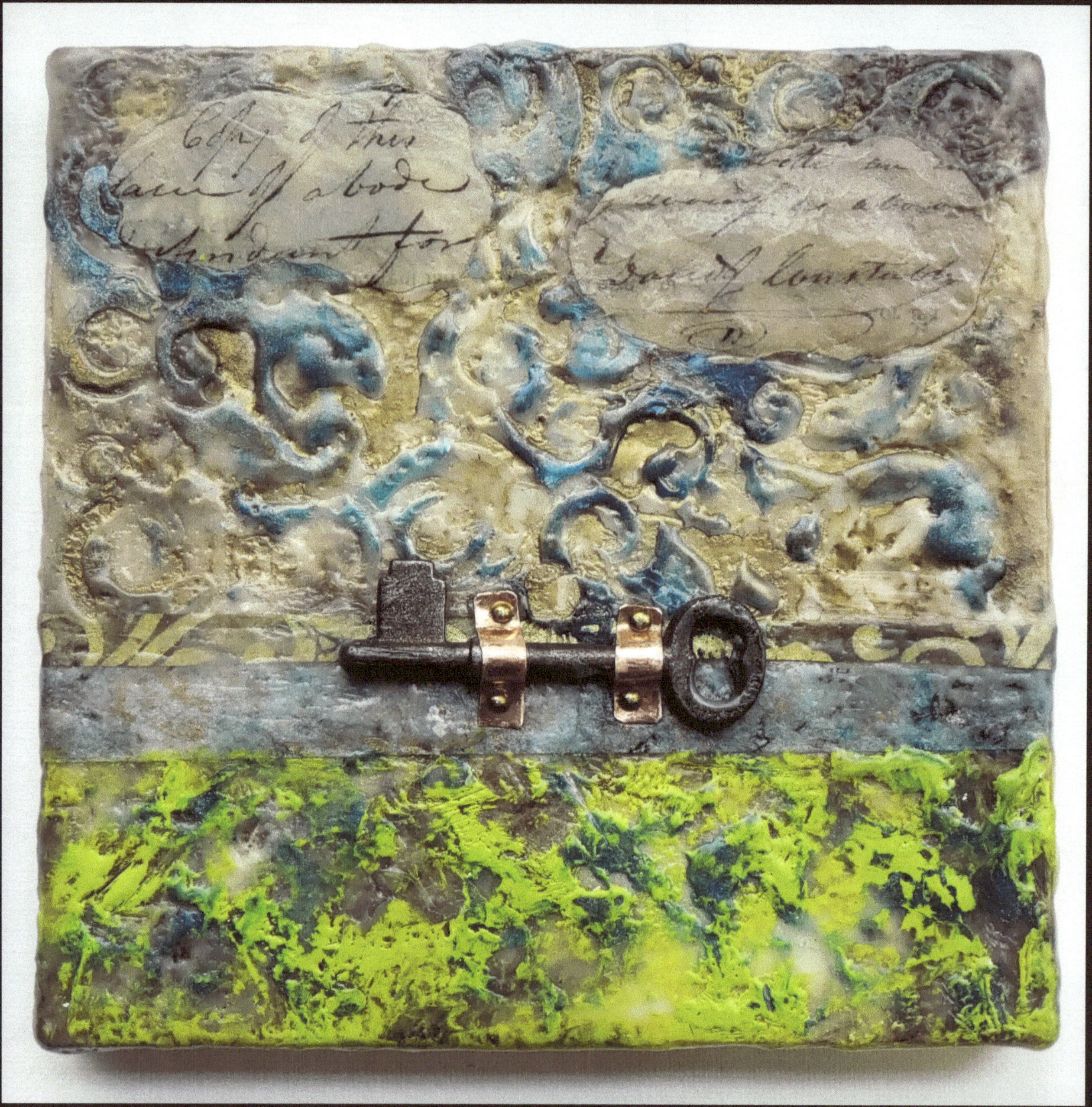

Gabrielle Zane, Solitudes Crowded With Loneliness, mixed media encaustic

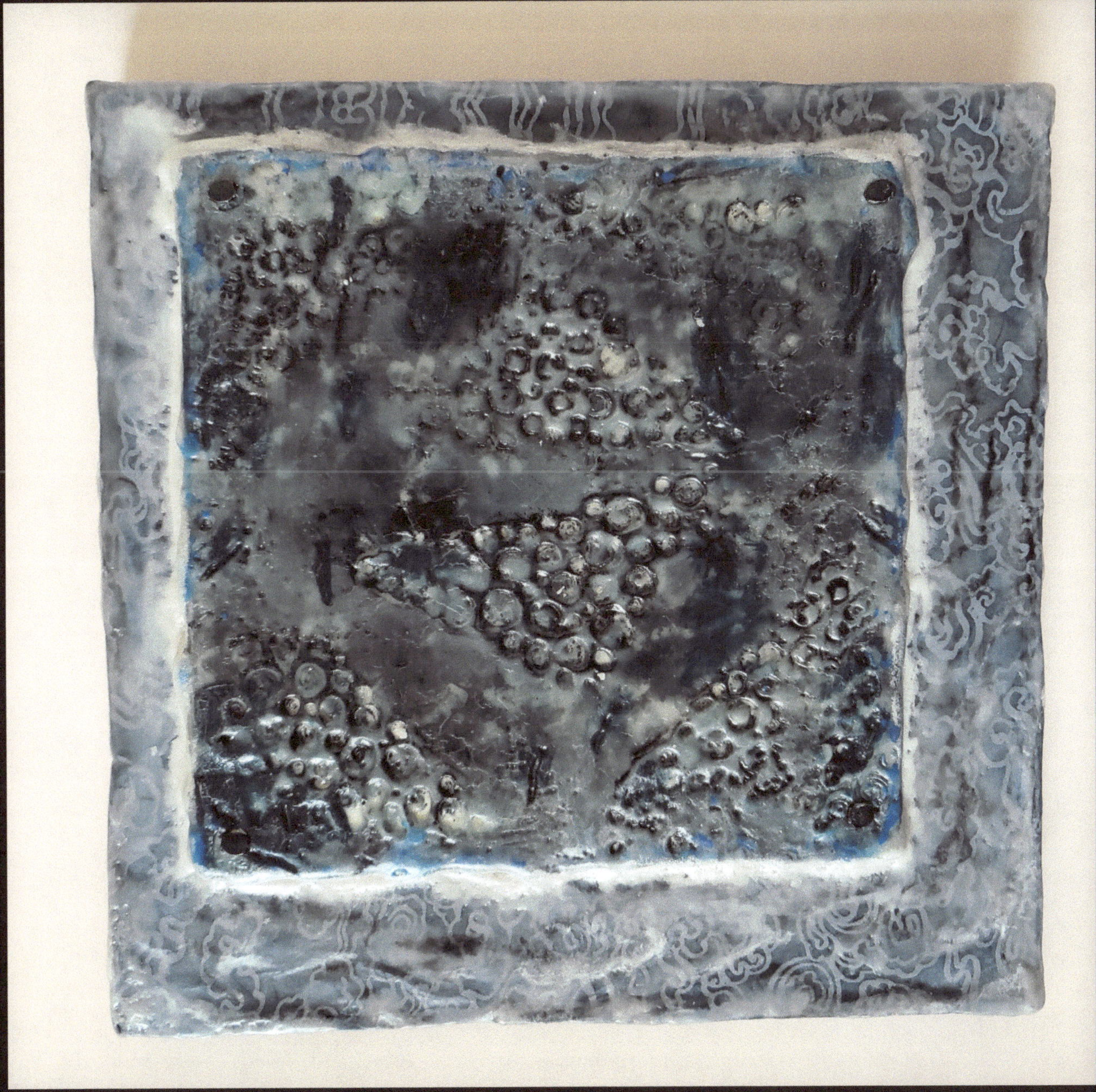

Gabrielle Zane, The Night Expands, mixed media encaustic

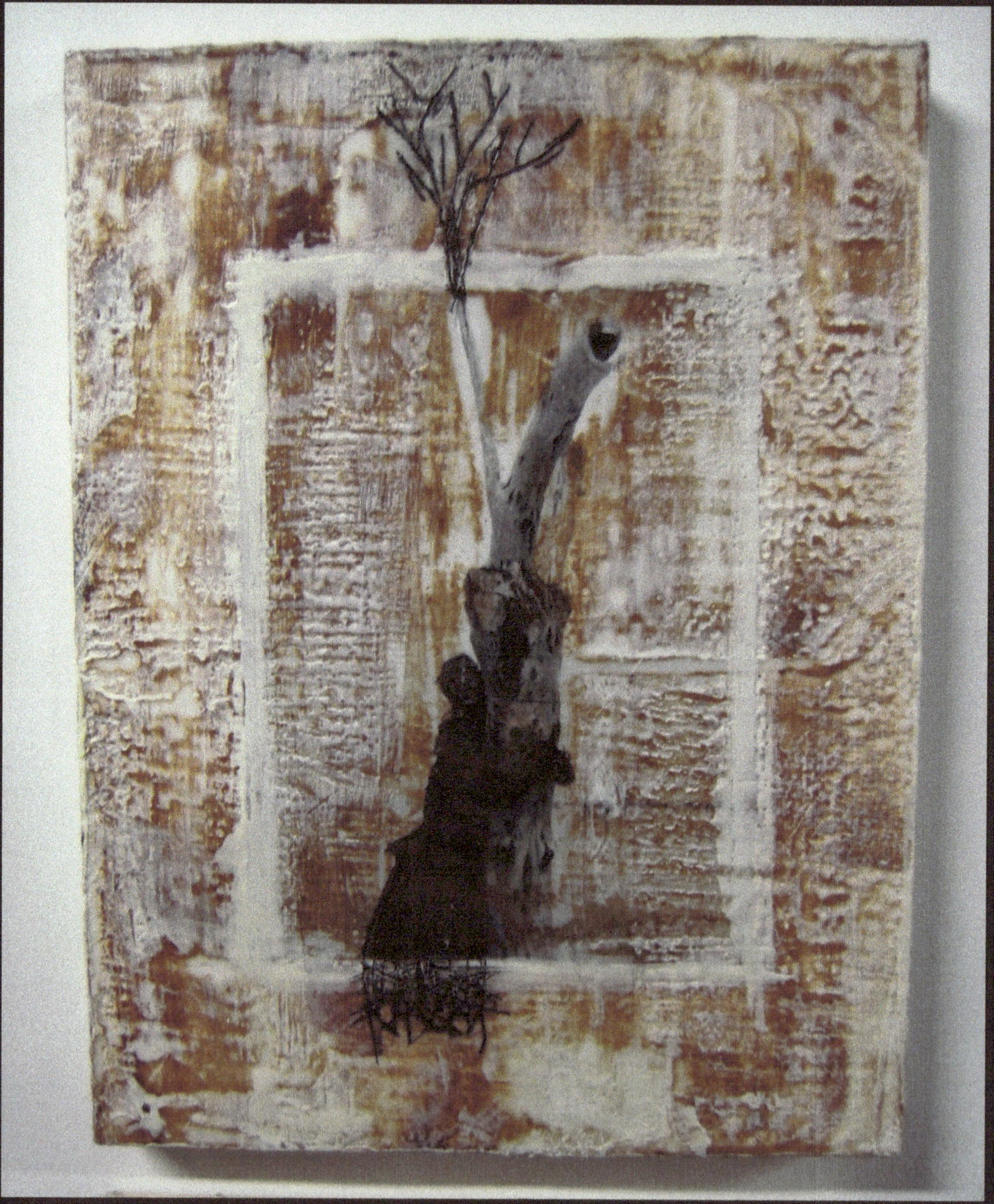

Gabrielle Zane, Unrequited, mixed media encaustic

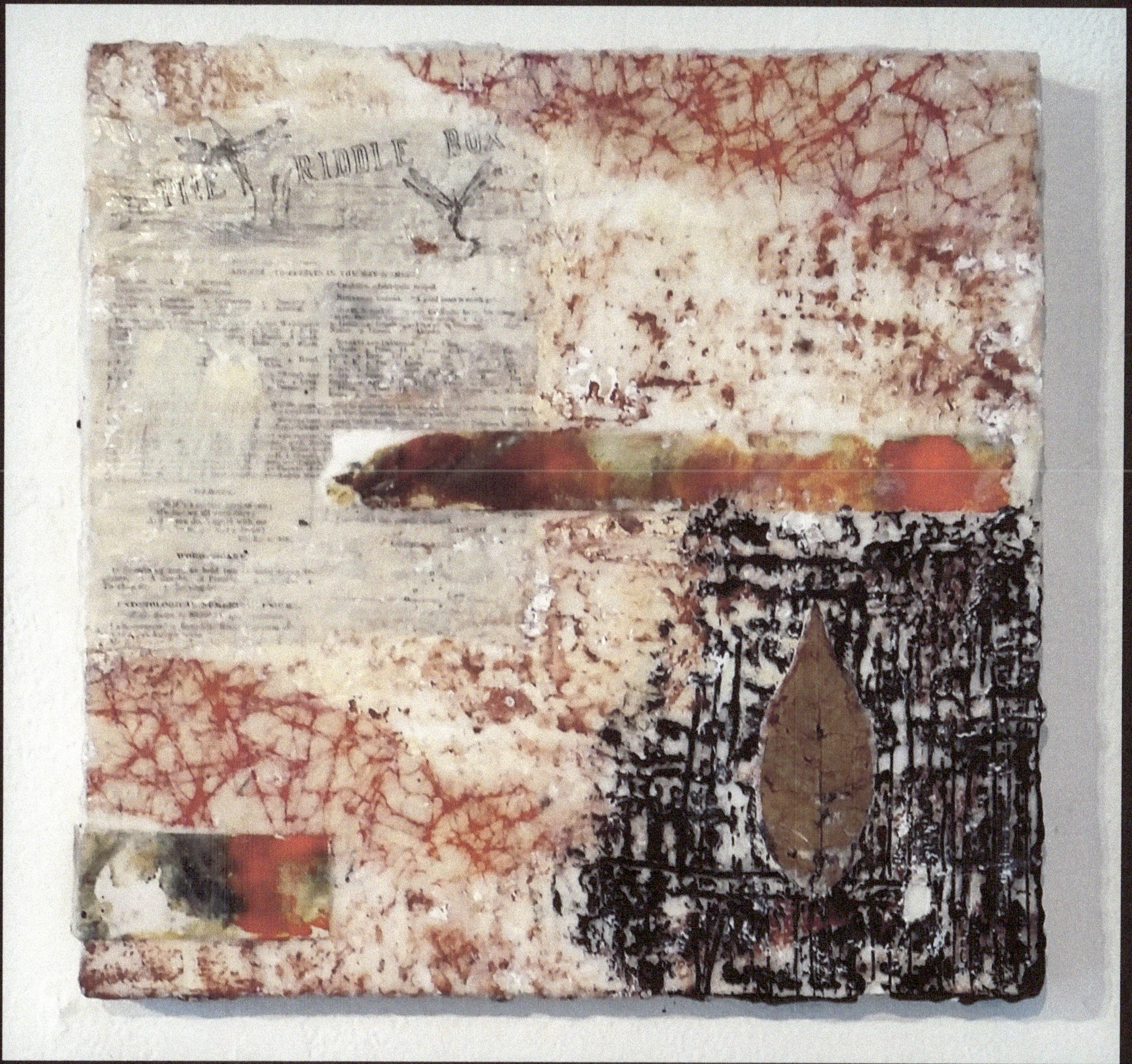

Gabrielle Zane, How We Learn From Our Mistakes, mixed media encaustic

Statements from the Artists

Debora Aldo

As a professional artist, I have been teaching art for four decades. My work is in public and private collections around the world. My personal work focuses on the destruction of natural marine and terrestrial habitats of our planet. (Pietreduredesign.com)

Glynis J. Blanker

There are those who take comfort in the fact that their bed sheets are the same color as the throw pillows, comforter, and curtains. Meaning there is a connection between them, an environment of order. Home for some is a place not only of comfort, but of control. This sense of order, in whatever form it takes, acts as a shield against the unpredictability and disorder of the outside world.

My images are an examination of the different forms this shield takes, and the thinking that lies behind it. I shoot familiar objects that are right in front of me, often creating a simplistic outcome of colors, shapes, and textures. For me, comfort and joy with a little control.

Virginia Chase

Intentional Camera Movement essentially consists of taking photographs by intentionally moving the camera to transcend reality and create another dimension in which sensations count more than facts; emotions more than evidence. (ICM) photography is an abstract style of shooting that has no rules – it all comes down to moving your camera over a long exposure.

Crystal ball, or lensball, photography is a creative technique that uses a glass ball to take an inverted image.

Glenn Alan Cheney

I have been a professional writer all my adult life, taking up painting only in the last few years. I wish I had started 50 years ago, though for some reason I don't think I would have been mature enough until recently. I don't know what maturity has to do with it, but it's a factor. And somehow the writing and painting talk to each other. There is a similarity, an overlap of technique, that I cannot define. Brevity of words, for example, translates to a certain kind of spaciousness on the canvas. Just the right word equals just the tiniest detail. I generally paint with acrylics but am trying to master oils. And I'm not trying to commit an act of art. I'm just going for pretty. (cheneybooks.com)

Karen Coombs

I balance my love of art with my love of nature. A graduate of Norwich Art School at Norwich Free Academy and the granddaughter of a local artist and gallery owner, I have spent years developing my artistic niche. My artistic style stems from my love of the New England coast and shows through my incorporation of elements from nature into each piece I create.

Rita Dawley

My work consists of both my inner and outer life. In retrospect, I have recognized it is an intimate portrayal of my journey.

I work on paper in a narrative form. My images appear to be exotic or tropical yet also include everyday life experiences. I choose to show these things, people, trees and animals in bright colors and design. There is an organized chaos in my work as there is in my life.

My expression or the mood of the night or day will be shown through emotive markings of color and images. There is also a quilt effect with primitive symbols and domesticated folk images and scenes. My narrative painting may confuse the casual observer as I use many worlds in one mind and put them on paper as a journey. I clearly reflect my emotions and moods through humor, whimsy, fantasy and color. I would hope the viewers might respond with their own imagination and primitive instincts of story telling while they cruise through mine.

Mark Dixon

Many of my images are of people or how people influence their environment. My training as a scientist helps me see details, understand relationships, and record information. I have worked hard at gaining a creative aesthetic to go with my observational skills. I prefer "in-situ" portraits. (markdixonphotography.com)

Michael Dubenetsky

I am a Norwich native who travels between Norwich and Boston and always has his camera with him. I started photography to fill my time when I retired from work. I love Street, Landscape, Flower, and Abstract photography. (facebook.com/MichaelDubenetsky)

Carol Dunn

Although I currently work primarily in mixed media and printmaking, my first love has always been photography. I layer images within Photoshop, and I love using apps to alter my images. I have recently started applying AI (Artificial Intelligence) to some of my images, which has opened up a whole new world of fun and experimentation. (caroldunnart.com)

Blaney Harris

I have been full time painting and teaching painting and drawing since retiring from the Navy in '94. I received my art training at Boston University School of Fine Arts back in the late '60s. I lived In Arizona for a while practicing my craft but as way leads to way, I joined the Navy and served on submarines. Today I have shifted to doing more abstract work, very much in the style of the Abstract Expressionists.

Sandra Jeknavorian

Slowing down and connecting with the world around me. Being fully present in the moment, whether big or small in significance. Doing what I want to do. Working with things I like, that inspire me. This is when I am truly living and this is what I strive to do as an artist. I alternate between different mediums and modes of working, prompting my mind to travel into different realms of thinking and feeling. Most of my source imagery originates from the natural world, then I allow my imagination to be my guide. I am happy when my artistic practice becomes a meditative experience. While some planning goes into my work, I never know what the end-result will be. The process is just as important as the end-product and I am excited by this mystery. As Robert Henri writes in The Art Spirit, "For an artist to be interesting to us they must have been interesting to themselves."

I earned my BFA in Painting with a minor in Art History at Hartford Art School and an MFA in Painting from the University of Massachusetts, Amherst. I am a professor of Painting and Drawing at Three Rivers Community College in Norwich, Connecticut. I have curated shows and exhibited my work widely on the east coast My work is part of the permanent collection of the United States Federal Government, Department of the State; two of my paintings are installed in the United States Embassy in Yerevan, Armenia. I am an elected artist at Norwich Arts Center and a member of Armenian International Women Artists. I reside in Connecticut with my husband, sculptor Sean Langlais and my son, Charlie.

Susan Scott Kenney

I live in the beautiful Last Green Valley, so my work reflects my local area–the local trails along the river, the changing of the seasons, the winter snows covering trees like frosting on a cake, spring beckoning with green buds and splashes of color as daffodils and tulips emerge. Summer on the New England coast brings sea, sand, and rocks. The brilliant colors of fall announce the approach of winter.

I work with acrylics and palette knives to represent the texture and color of the world around us, inviting the viewer to see it with me. I hope my paintings bring as much joy and peace to others as they do to me. (susanscottkenney.com)

Melody Knight Leary

Working out of my home-based studio in Norwich, Conn., I'm a practicing artist whose preferred mode of creative expression is printmaking. I work in a variety of printmaking media with a focus on less toxic materials and processes. After a long and rewarding teaching career, I now focus on my own studio practice. I often think of myself as a visual narrator who enjoys complexity, implied meaning, and layering and I take pleasure in pairing and grouping images to express feelings, ideas and emotions. What I'm aiming for is a print that might touch people, provide a point for connection, and offer a moment of contemplation. I exhibit throughout the US and abroad. My work is held in a number of private and public collections, a few of which include the Slater Memorial Museum, Casa de las Americas, Havana, Cuba, and University City Art Museum of Guangzhou Academy of Fine Arts in China.

Gerlinde Lehner

Creating, working with my hands, exploring a variety of mediums is my oasis. Be it fabric, paper or paint creating art leads me on a curious adventure. At first it starts with the inspiration that I have received from so many wonderful art instructors, then the exploration- with the hope of mastering the medium, and then finally the deeper exploration to make it my own. I continue to be inspired, to remain curious, and to continue the art-making adventure.

My personal inspiration is rounded out by being an avid gardener, living on the fringes of the ocean and the land. The natural world has shaped me, and it reflects in my work. As I look around and see the subtle colors blending of the chartreuse colored moss on a dark basalt rock, or the textures created by the smooth round beach stones; my eyes drink all of this beauty in, translating it eventually into my art.

Recently retired I am able to devote more time in the studio. Currently I am exploring dolls as a representation of self, book-making, and mixed media. (Gerlinde_lehner@comcast.net)

Mary Ann Lewis

I am a retired software developer. While still working, I found that digital photography was a pursuit that let me express myself creatively, and I actually enjoyed processing images on my computer. After retiring, I recently picked up my pencil and paintbrush after many years of not having time to spend drawing and painting. I have used my photos as subjects for my drawings and paintings, and I feel as though I have come full circle. When not working on images at home, I can often be found hiking in the woods with my dog Brooke and a camera.

Gabe Lipman

My daughter-in-law describes us as a "family of makers". That description suits me just fine. I've been cutting, gluing, coloring, drawing, painting, printing (all this making) since I was a small child. Clearly, it's what I am most experienced in.

In my work I invite you into my view of the world. It is a world of moments captured in a place, or a view that stirred something in me which I remember over and over again, even though the moment is fleeting.

I have retained a catalog of visual images collected in my brain - a series of colors, a particular sky against the water, the horizon, rolling hills along the Hudson River, the gorgeous autumn colors seen driving through Pennsylvania, a magenta tree in a garden center in Virginia, or the kissing trees in the Roman Forum. These images have evoked a remembrance of calm, serenity, foreboding, beauty, or majesty.

My work is created using my current favorite materials: chalk pastel or oil pastel. All are works on paper. I like it when my hands are dirty with the colors I've used, and then my sink is full of those colors as I wash my hands. To me the doing (the making) is as important as the finished piece - in fact maybe more.

Susan Masse

I am a retired graphic artist who loves having time to create art. I studied painting at the Old Lyme Academy and Connecticut College. Although I am keeping my graphic skills honed, I am thrilled to be producing art again. I have not "fixed" on a style yet and am eager to see where I go next. My work is generally "quiet" but can exhibit a playful streak.

Lori Neumann

An artist and a teacher, I enjoy all forms of art, especially when it is created with natural fiber from sheep and angora goats raised on the farm! Trained in fine arts at the Lyme Academy in Lyme, CT, I especially enjoy oil painting and working with fiber which I regularly exhibit & sell both locally and out of state. I began working with animal fiber and needle felting almost ten years ago. Needle felting is the process of forming natural and dyed wool into a solid shape or fabric by tangling it together with a special barbed needle or agitating the fiber with soap & water. Felting can be used to create both a three-dimensional shape such as an animal or bird or used to create wool "tapestry" style paintings in two-dimensions. It is a very diverse art form which also includes "wet felting" to create apparel items such as a scarf or hand warmers.

I maintain a farm with horses, sheep, goats, chickens, a donkey, and a pig, and I try to utilize their fiber in my art, from wool to tail hair and dropped feathers! I love to share & teach the love of art and believe that within each of us there is an artist, waiting to be released! (menageriebylori.com)

Marianne Nicholas

I have always been mesmerized by the forest as well as the ocean, these realms are where I find the beauty that sparks my inspiration to create. While I would love to only stick to paint, brushes, and canvases in my studio, all mediums excite me and when I incorporate collage materials I think it feels raw and somehow complete. I love experimenting with fabric and stitching and will continue to let this evolve in my paintings.

Susan Parish

My work has evolved over the years from the traditional black and white darkroom to being fully digital. I enjoy the immediacy of the photos from the digital camera. Photoshop gives me amazing control over the final images. My output is on an Epson Sure Color P800 printer.

In my subject matter I look for "evidence of humans," though I rarely include people in my work. I tend to gather photographs into series; public bathrooms, things in 3's, photos including words, things that are painted etc. I have also traveled to Mexico for the past twenty years to photograph.

Mark Patnode

Why not throw it, sling it, splash it? It's the artist's mark – it's Mark-Making^{TM}.

I strive for powerful visual simplicity in my artwork. The first marks establish a relationship with the subject and it becomes a dialog as I develop the work. Working quickly and with great intensity, I create the poetry of the transitory moment.

Though I paint a variety of subjects, I find great satisfaction working with landscapes and cityscapes. I feel the light from the sky influences everything because I sense it as not above but all around. The more I study nature the more I arrive at a language of form and color - yet I want my application to be as far removed from nature as possible. I want to feel free with paint and don't want to be constrained with convention. (junerandmark.com)

Yujuan Patnode

What is an artist? I feel it is to use your hands to describe the seemingly ordinary but beautiful moments in life. To use your eyes to help others discover details they cannot see. To record your feelings in your special way. So I train hard as I want my hands to be like those of a craftsman. I want my eyes to be like a child. I want my sensitivity to emulate the wings of a butterfly.

The origin of Chinese characters is painting. There are many excellent parts of Chinese culture that many other cultures are not aware of. I want everyone to understand it, so I choose to paint more as a science - in the Chinese way. I feel this is my mission to paint now. (junerandmark.com and lizhaiarts.com)

Lori Rembetski

My ceramic sculpture and tiles are influenced by a love of animals and nature. I am inspired by patterns and shapes that I observe while walking my dog around the neighborhood or through the woods. My goal is to evoke the feeling of joy I find in nature.

Lisa Shasha

I would rather draw than eat, I love it so much. Other activities that fill my life with joy and purpose are singing, writing, playing the piano, and acting. I have improved vastly as an artist on account of my involvement with Norwich Arts Center that began over six years ago. My aspiration after my own show of abstracts at the Wauregan art gallery is to branch out to galleries in Boston.

Gretchen van der Lyke

My work confronts issues of grief and recovery through the drama of organic forms. Botanical art has been a dominant foundational influence.

In addition my parents are both avid antique collectors. As a result, I grew up among the various aesthetics of earlier times. I believe this has lent a soft and handcrafted quality to my work.

I majored in Art and Art History at Clark University. I also have a Certificate of Decorative Painting from R.I.S.D

My most commonly used media is Watercolor, and sometimes Chalk Pastel. In recent years, my work has veered into Collage techniques. I love to explore the plasticity of paper, blurring the line between Sculpture and Painting.

I have always lived in the New London County area, the local plants and seasonal rhythms of southeast New England influence my work. (gvanderlyke.blogspot.com)

Gabrielle Zane

As a Teaching Artist for the Connecticut Commission on Culture & Tourism, I've been an artist-in-residence in schools throughout New England. I hold an MFA from Bennington College. I founded and coordinated the NAC Kids After School Arts Program from 2003- 2009. I'm a member of Moulton Court Artists, Norwich Arts Cooperative, and CAFA. Using encaustic, photography and multi-media, my work explores the realms of connection - how our striving for intimacy affects our relationships to ourselves, others, nature, and the world around us. I attempt to evoke a sense of how the "ordinary" things in life can bring us to larger truths of the struggle between fulfillment and longing, grasping and letting go, and the transitory nature of our experiences. I like to create pieces that include natural elements, photographs, letters, old books, illustrations, metal and 3-D objects, to create a feeling of mystery and surrealism. My studio, "Waxing Moon" is at 31 Moulton Court, Willimantic, Conn. (facebook.com/WaxingMoonStudio)

Norwich Arts Center

Norwich Arts Center was formed in 1987 as the Norwich Arts Council. The founders were a group of local artists and arts-lovers who were inspired by the region's cultural possibilities. The mission was and is to provide affordable programming in a variety of arts that reflects the area's rich diversity and deepens arts appreciation.

The Center was first known as Norwich Artists Co-Op. The cooperation began with a group of artists refurbishing the main gallery space with sheetrock and paint. They encouraged more artists to apply for membership, and they took turns opening the gallery to the public and providing refreshments for opening receptions.

NAC is still an all-volunteer non-profit organization located in downtown Norwich at 60-64 Broadway. Two galleries at street level exhibit paintings, sculptures, and other works. The 100-seat Donald L. Oat Theater, on the third floor, presents theater, films, and musical performances. The second floor is rented as individual offices.

Members are the core of the organization. Elected artists, chosen by democratic jury for their qualifications, are the primary volunteers, and do all the work necessary for running the galleries. Their work is exhibited in solo shows on a rotating basis. Associate artists and all artists have a variety of opportunities to exhibit their works by entering any of the 6 or more exhibits during the year, which sometimes have a theme, and for which prizes are awarded. Gallery Too also offers artisan crafts such as jewelry and greeting cards.

Exhibits in the galleries change monthly, with receptions on the evenings of First Fridays. Visit NorwichArts.org for more information and to sign up for news, event schedules, and volunteer opportunities.

New London Librarium

New London Librarium is a literary press in Hanover, Conn. It specializes in books that merit publication but are unlikely to achieve the sales expected by larger publishers. NLL publishes a wide variety of books, some in series on Catholic issues, environmental issues, Brazil, history, art, and general interest. Several titles are translations of Brazilian classics. For more information, see NLLibrarium.com.

www.ingramcontent.com/pod-product-compliance
Lightning Source LLC
Chambersburg PA
CBHW051912210526
45473CB00006B/1987